DIVERSITY IN AGING

Edited by

Scott A. Bass, Elizabeth A. Kutza, and Fernando M. Torres-Gil

Foreword by Ken Dychtwald

PROFESSIONAL BOOKS ON AGING
SCOTT, FORESMAN AND COMPANY
GLENVIEW, ILLINOIS LONDON

The editors wish to thank Carolinda Douglas, Jeff Hyde, A. Jean Lesher, Jill R. Norton, and James O'Brien for their invaluable assistance with this book.

The authors of Chapter 2 wish to express special appreciation to Ms. Amy Chung of Self-Help for the Elderly of San Francisco for her insights into the needs of the elderly of that city. Special thanks also to Dr. L.C. Dorsey of the Delta Health Center of Mound Bayou, Mississippi, for her analysis of the problems of the rural elderly in Mississippi. And finally, thanks to Ms. Barbara Brodbar of the staff of the Southeast Florida Center on Aging, who contributed her substantial practice experience to analyzing and editing the case material.

Library of Congress Cataloging-in-Publication Data

Diversity in aging : challenges facing the White House Conference on Aging / edited by Scott A. Bass, Elizabeth A. Kutza, Fernando M. Torres-Gil.
p. cm.—(Professional books on aging)
Includes bibliographical references.
ISBN 0-673-24933-6
1. Aged—United States—Social conditions. 2. Aged—Government policy—United States. I. Bass, Scott A. II. Kutza, Elizabeth A. III. Torres-Gil, Fernando M. IV. Series.
HQ1064.U5D58 1989
305.26'0973—dc20 89-10783
CIP

1 2 3 4 5 6 KPF 94 93 92 91 90 89

ISBN 0-673-24933-6

Printed in the United States of America.

Scott, Foresman professional books are available for bulk sales at quantity discounts. For information, please contact Marketing Manager, Professional Books Group, Scott, Foresman and Company, 1900 East Lake Avenue, Glenview, IL 60025.

Foreword

Until this century, most people didn't grow old—they died. Our ancestors could only dream of seven, eight, or nine decades of life. Although most of us now take it for granted that we will live this long, the idea of mass longevity is relatively new: Two-thirds of all the men and women who have ever lived to the age of 65 or beyond in the entire history of the world are alive today. The elderly men and women all around us are the social pioneers of a grand new era in human evolution.

With declining fertility rates and rising life expectancies, our demographic composition is shifting, and shifting rapidly. Our youth-oriented culture, which has for most of this century attempted to ignore or avoid issues pertaining to the aging of the population, is about to come face to face with its own aging process.

Not only are more of us growing older, we're doing so in new and different ways. Today's older men and women are living with a great deal more health, vigor, social independence, financial security, and political clout than any previous generation. And this trend toward a more powerful old age is destined to continue as the baby boomers migrate into life's second half.

During the past half century since the initial rumblings of "gray power" and the initiation of Social Security in the 1930s, senior advocacy groups have grown with astonishing speed. Today they include:

- 20,000 seniors in the Older Women's League (OWL);
- 74,000 in the fiercely activist Gray Panthers, with chapters in thirty states;
- 2.2 million in the conservative National Alliance of Senior Citizens (NASC);
- 4.5 million in the 4,000 local chapters of the National Council of Senior Citizens (NCSC), founded by the AFL-CIO;
- 30 million members in the American Association of Retired Persons (AARP), which has seen its membership skyrocket since its 1958 founding.

The growth of this kind of organized, seasoned activism is unrivaled by any other population segment or special interest group.

The federal budget shows the same growth in the clout of the elderly. Before 1935 almost no funds were earmarked specifically for the elderly. In the most recent budget, however, federal subsidies for housing, meals, medical care, federal pensions, Social Security, and other benefits for the elderly comprised nearly 28 percent of the budget, roughly equal to the amount spent on defense.

However, despite all these helpful programs, the transition to a social policy that supports a vital and productive old age is still occurring in an alarmingly *uneven* fashion.

One of the most prevalent myths surrounding old age in the United States is that there is only one way of being old, and that most older people think, feel, act, and look pretty much the same—and therefore have similar needs. Although most of us recognize, even celebrate, the vast diversity of youth, we tend to lump all 30 million Americans who are over 65 as "the elderly." And by using that label, we suggest that the elderly are more alike than different.

When we look beyond the myth, as I have come to realize during the fifteen years that I have been studying America's elderly, no age group is more varied in personal background, physical abilities, personal styles, social needs, or financial capabilities than today's older population. In fact, research has repeatedly proven that in their later years people become more, not less, diverse.

Perhaps in earlier eras, the few people who lived to advanced old age could have been described by common traits and may well have shared many common experiences. But today, when one in eight Americans is over the age of 65 and when forty years and three generations may separate the younger from the older "elderly," sweeping generalizations are inappropriate.

Today's older Americans are a symphony of cultural diversity. Many came to America during the flood of immigration in the early years of this century. They have roots in Poland or China, in Ireland, Greece, or Japan; they are likely to have less in common with each other than do their children. Each age (from 65 to 100), gender, race, and ethnic group has distinctive characteristics.

Some older people are dreadfully sick and waiting for death. Some are fit and training for marathons. Some wait in breadlines for a warm meal. Others have condos in Vail and yachts in Tahiti.

Some older people live rigidly conservative life-styles; other are extremely free-spirited. Some retirees feel finished with their careers and are happy to putter in the garden, travel, and volunteer. Others love their work and hope to pursue it as long as they can.

At the same moment that some older men and women are experiencing their greatest pleasures and satisfactions, others are suffering through a nightmare of illness, poverty, and despair. And while existing government programs are not needed at all by some older men and women, other elderly persons are profoundly underserved by the current offerings.

Any age group has these divergences, these extremes. What is astonishing about the elderly is that the extremes are expanding as the homogeneous center diminishes.

There is every indication that America in the 1990s and the twenty-first century will be even more striking in its diversity. Tomorrow's elders will most likely be different not only from one another but from today's elders as well. The world is changing so fast that each generation is, in some ways, increasingly different from the ones that came before. In the past fifty years we have entered the atomic age, the space age, and the computer age; life expectancy has increased by more than fifteen years; more than eighty new nations have appeared worldwide; and the global population has more than doubled. It is thought that 75 percent of the information ever known in the history of the world has been discovered in the last twenty-five years.

With this rate of change, tomorrow's elderly will have little in common with yesterday's. They will have traveled farther, read more, met more people, lived through more world changes, experienced more sexual and life-style experimentation, lived longer, and taken part in a more powerful "gerontocracy" than any previous generation.

Perhaps the next major challenge is to revisit the needs and concerns underlying today's programs and see how well they meet the needs of tomorrow's aging America. Some programs have probably served their initial purposes and should be trimmed back or eliminated. At the same time, there is no doubt that many new and innovative strategies will be required to meet the complex intergenerational challenges of the coming decades.

This is the message emphasized in *Diversity in Aging: Challenges Facing the White House Conference on Aging*. Data presented in this book by America's seminal thinkers and visionaries paint a portrait of increasing ethnic diversity, a greater variety of life-styles, and a broader range of incomes among the elderly than ever before.

This diversity is not merely an interesting social phenomenon. It has implications for social policy and programs. *Diversity in Aging* directs itself to these more pragmatic political and practical issues as well, by offering enlightening examinations of how social institutions can respond to such diversity. The authors suggest that the next White House Conference on Aging may provide the opportunity to plan for this diversity on a national scale.

This book should be read by public officials, service providers, and advocates of the elderly—in short, by all those who are committed to ensuring that diversity in our older population is recognized, allowed for, and responded to in as exciting and appropriate a manner as possible.

Ken Dychtwald
Chairman and CEO
Age Wave, Inc.

Contents

Contributors

Scott A. Bass, Ph.D., is director of the Gerontology Institute, University of Massachusetts at Boston, and an associate professor and chair of the gerontology department at the University's College of Public and Community Service. He is one of the founders of its Gerontology Certificate Program, a national model for the teaching of students over 60 years old about aging and social policy. He has written extensively on the subject and is co-editor of *Retirement Reconsidered: Social and Economic Roles for Older People* (with Robert Morris).

Robert H. Binstock, Ph.D., is the Henry R. Luce Professor of Aging, Health, and Society at the School of Medicine, Case Western Reserve University, in Cleveland, Ohio. A former president of the Gerontological Society of America (1975 to 1976), he has also served as director of a White House Task Force on Older Americans (1967 to 1968). He is the author of *Feasible Planning for Social Change, The Politics of the Powerless,* and *America's Political System* (four editions), and editor of the *Handbook of Aging and the Social Sciences* (two editions).

Ken Dychtwald, Ph.D., is chairman and chief executive officer of Age Wave, Inc., a consulting firm formed in 1986 to inform and educate businesses, institutions, and government about the implications of an aging population. He serves as a special correspondent on aging issues for CBS News and is the author of five books including *Age Wave,* published in 1989.

Mimi Kmet is currently western editor for Gralla Publications. She is a writer and editor for various industry and trade journals. She received her B.A. in journalism from the University of Southern California, where she was also an editorial assistant at the Andrus Gerontology Center.

Sanford L. Kravitz, Ph.D., is currently Distinguished Professor of Public Affairs at Florida International University in Miami and senior consultant to the University's Southeast Florida Center on Aging. He has had a forty-year career in social work, serving as dean of the School of Social Work at City University of New York—Stony Brook and as associate director of the War on Poverty's Community Action Program. During his tenure with the Office of Economic Opportunity, he was responsible for organizing the Foster Grandparents Program, the Neighborhood Health Center programs, Upward Bound, and a score of other programs.

Elizabeth Ann Kutza, Ph.D., is associate professor and director of the Institute on Aging at the School of Urban and Public Affairs, Portland State University, Portland, Oregon. Before that appointment, she was on the faculty of the University of Chicago for ten years. She is the author of *The Benefits of Old Age: Social Welfare Policy for the Elderly* and has written widely on long-term care and community-based aging services. As a Robert Wood Johnson Health Policy Fellow from 1983 to 1984, Dr. Kutza served as a professional staff member of the Senate Finance Committee in Washington, D.C.

Harry R. Moody, Ph.D., is deputy director of the Brookdale Center on Aging of Hunter College, City University of New York, where he has been since 1975. He is the author of the book *Abundance of Life: Human Development Policies for an Aging Society.* He has published more than forty articles on lifelong learning, social policy, and bioethics and is now completing a book on bioethics and aging.

Martha B. Pelaez, Ph.D., is the associate director of the Southeast Florida Center on Aging of Florida International University in Miami. She is responsible for developing gerontology training programs for professionals working in the aging advocacy network throughout Southeast Florida.

Max B. Rothman, J.D., is the executive director of the Southeast Florida Center on Aging, Florida International University. His specialty is state organizational and policy issues in long-term care. He served for eight years as Florida's district administrator for all state human services in Dade and Monroe counties. Before that, he directed three legal services programs and served both as a Peace Corps Volunteer in Venezuela and as a trainer.

Cynthia Taeuber has been a demographic specialist at the Bureau of the Census since 1974. She has written extensively on women, the current older population, and implications of the aging of the baby-boom generation. Her major publications include *America in Transition: An Aging Society, Demographic Dimensions of an Aging Society* (with J.S. Siegel), *America's Oldest Old* (with Ira Rosenwaike), *America's Centenarians* (with G. Spencer and A. Goldstein), *An Aging World* (with B. Torrey and K. Kinsella), and *Women in the American Economy* (with V. Valdisera).

Fernando M. Torres-Gil, Ph.D., is associate professor of gerontology and public administration at the University of Southern California in Los Angeles. He has served as staff director of the U.S. House Select Committee on Aging and as special assistant to former Secretaries of Health and Human Services Joseph Califano and Patricia Harris. He has also been a policy advisor on aging and health care to several congressional and presidential candidates. He is currently president of the American Society on Aging.

INTRODUCTION

Diversity in Aging: The Challenges Facing the White House Conference on Aging

SCOTT A. BASS, ELIZABETH ANN KUTZA,
AND FERNANDO M. TORRES-GIL

The graying of the major industrial nations is upon us, and we have just begun to grapple with its implications. In the next century, one of every four persons in the United States—that is, nearly one in every three adults—may be 65 years old or older. The growing numbers of older persons, with their dramatically increasing life expectancies, has spurred the expansion of programs and services targeted to the aged and their families. More generally, public policy toward the elderly has become a constant concern for beneficiaries, taxpayers, policymakers, and elected officials.

Our goal in this book is to point out to a wide audience—planners, policymakers, elderly advocates, journalists, academics, family members, elected officials, students—that *the programmatic strategies of the past twenty years, in all likelihood, will be unresponsive to the dramatically changing needs of the population and to the political climate of the 1990s and beyond.* This book is designed to help us better understand how different today's elderly are from the elderly of the past, and how the diversity among them will increase in the relatively near future. The book presents ways in which to rethink our strategies for programs for the elderly and their families, and in doing so points to new directions for the future.

We hope that it will help to start what is certain to be a long debate on the future of policies on aging in America, triggering more detailed plans and models during the next White House Conference on Aging and at other forums involving those concerned with services and programs for our aging society.

Understanding Our Diverse Elderly

In the rapid transition to an aging society, we often seem to look on the "elderly" as a nameless and faceless mass of persons whose age bracket—65 years and older—somehow gives all of them the same needs and same wants. In our need to come to grips with the aging of our society, we too often take it for granted that the elderly are alike in background, needs, and experience. We grasp at pat descriptions and labels that are easily and quickly communicated in referring to the aging population.

This view of the elderly as a homogeneous group is widely held, and not only by the nonelderly. Even senior citizen groups in the United States often pursue their interests as if they represented a constituency with one common agenda. In pursuit of this agenda the elderly are frequently portrayed as frail, sick, and dependent. In the literature on aging, which reflects the professions that serve the elderly, it is these images of dependency that predominate. In reality, some elders are in need of extensive medical and support services, but most are not.

For several decades this "rocking-chair" image of older people has been a dominant stereotype. It has been fiercely resisted by groups in the United States such as the Gray Panthers, whose media watch program has increased the public's awareness of the derogatory images of older people. More recently, however, the popular press in the United States has begun to present another image, equally damaging and no more accurate; this image depicts the elderly as affluent jet-setters who are preoccupied with their own material needs. Insulting labels such as "greedy geezers" have been used to describe today's aged.

Real life, of course, is not as simple and easily understood as popular culture would have us think. The elderly are not either rich or poor, greedy or needy, independent or dependent; they fit all and none and some of the above descriptions. Many providers and volunteers working with the elderly have long recognized vast differences among them. Programs based on the assumption that all elders are alike may unintentionally exclude many of those who need help the most. Unfortunately, overgeneralizations of the elderly can all too quickly lead to false assumptions and misguided solutions—all in the name of doing right for the elderly.

The United States, more than any other nation with a rapidly aging population, is already extraordinarily diverse. Its people differ by race, ethnicity, language, education, socioeconomic status, geographic region, religion, life-style, and political and sexual persuasions. And we, like other nations, have become more diverse, not less, in recent decades. In this circumstance, why should we expect the 65-and-older group to be any less diverse than the society as a whole?

That huge 65-and-older age group includes elders in their nineties as well as recent retirees who may be some thirty years their junior. It joins those who are hale and hearty with those who have lived for years with disabilities, and it includes both rich and poor. Some older people run marathons, climb mountains, play golf, and compete in tennis. Some continue their careers as authors, scientists, and artists. Certain individuals, such as Frank Lloyd Wright, have produced their greatest works in their seventies and beyond. At the same time others may suffer from debilitating illnesses such as Alzheimer's disease, arthritis, or any of a host of other chronic disabilities. And for older people who grew up in locations as different as rural Mexico or urban New York, or with different educational backgrounds, the aging experience may be perceived very differently.

The awareness that all older persons are not alike is only now beginning to permeate the public and political consciousnesses. But, if we are to prepare for the aging of the society and minimize social dislocation, political polarization, and economic instability, we must understand the diversity of our aging population and how to respond to it. How do we ensure that diversity enriches our society rather than divides it? How can government at all levels respond flexibly to the myriad of differences in its older populations? How do we develop services that are sensitive to the cultural traditions of different immigrant and ethnic groups? And what role does academic research provide in understanding a diverse aged population? Diversity will go to the heart of political debates about such issues as bilingualism, age integration and segregation, cultural pluralism, and means-testing. We must understand where that diversity creates opportunities and where it leads to problems and tensions.

The White House Conference on Aging that is projected for the early 1990s may provide an opportunity to come to terms with the ramifications of diversity in our aging society. Previous conferences were important milestones in our country's attempt to understand and respond to the phenomenon of aging. They led to new thinking about what it means to be old and how government should respond to the needs of its elders. In two instances (1961 and 1971) the White House conferences produced major developments in public policies and benefits for the elderly. And in every instance, the conferences reflected important and largely positive responses to the changes expected during the decade ahead. The next White House Conference on Aging, too, should be prepared to take up the most compelling issues facing our aging society.

Diversity and White House Conferences on Aging

The 1990s will be a crucial time in the changing demography of the United States. The rapid growth of older persons will stabilize temporarily, just before the twenty-first century brings the largest group of elderly. The "baby boomers" will be in their most productive years in the 1990s, contributing their talents to economic growth. Major entitlement programs such as Social Security will remain solvent. Therefore, from the 1990s until about 2010 represents a window of opportunity to prepare for a dramatically diverse nation in the next century and a much larger and more diverse older population.

The first National Conference on Aging, under President Harry Truman, brought together service providers and community-level volunteers. While it did not result in major, concrete achievements, it did raise expectations of future high-level consideration of aging issues. It set the stage for the 1961 White House Conference on Aging, which was noteworthy for its major health debates. Groups such as the American Federation of Labor and Congress of Industrial Organizations (AFL-CIO), the newly developed American Association of Retired Persons (AARP), and National Council on Aging (NCOA) viewed the 1961 conference as an opportunity to argue for health care for the elderly. Historians now partly credit the passage of Medicare and Medicaid in 1965 to the public awareness and organizing stimulated at the White House Conference four years earlier.

The 1971 conference made aging a public issue and established the credibility of the elderly, through organizations such as the AARP, NCOA, the National Council of Senior Citizens (NCSC), as advocates for their own needs. It signaled the political maturity of older persons. More important, in its aftermath there came major expansions of public benefits and services for the elderly, many of which were promised by President Nixon at the conference's closing session.

The 1981 White House Conference on Aging, perhaps, is best remembered for what it did *not* accomplish. Planned by President Carter's administration and carried out by President Reagan's, it was notable for its political turmoil. It did not result in new policies or the expansion of benefits. However, it did galvanize senior organizations in opposing dramatic cutbacks in their programs. In fact, seniors were successful throughout the 1980s in protecting Social Security, Medicare, and the Older Americans Act.

The next White House Conference on Aging will not have to concern itself with raising public awareness about aging issues, as did the first one during the Truman administration. And, despite the political influence of the elderly, delegates will not have the luxury of recommending major new programs, as did their counterparts in 1961 and 1971. The federal deficit and Congress's reluctance to increase taxes have narrowed the playing field. On the other hand, the next conference will not have to face the political conflicts of 1981, since it will be planned and implemented essentially by the same administration.

The next conference will need to address the social, political, economic, and demographic changes affecting our society. This book argues that the next conference—and our thinking and planning in the next decade—should be about change, and should use diversity as an overarching context within which to examine such issues as long-term care, intergenerational relationships, Social Security, and retirement policies. The chapters of this book all subscribe to the premise that we must look *beyond* the 1990s, and that we must concern ourselves with those who will be elderly during the early part of the next century. Those who will be alive in the early twenty-first century, including many of today's elderly, will live with the consequences of how we respond to their and our diversity.

It is to that end that this book explores diversity and its implications for the future—beyond the next White House Conference on Aging. It is not meant to serve as a road map or to chart specific directions or recommendations, however; that is the job for delegates to the next conference on aging and for advocates for the elderly. Rather, the editors have sought to present a number of the issues whose resolution, or lack of it, will have significant implications for us all.

The first chapter, by Cynthia Taeuber, provides a detailed description of exactly how diverse the current population is and how much *more* diverse it will be in the future. Sanford Kravitz, Martha Pelaez, and Max Rothman in Chapter 2 address the immediate impact of diversity on the providers, practitioners, and recipients of services for the elderly. They also discuss the "bureaucratic" and organizational issues in providing these services.

Do older persons represent a monolithic political bloc or simply a "political bluff"? Can the current political focus of aging interest groups truly respond to an increasingly diverse aging population? These are the questions framed by Robert H. Binstock in Chapter 3, as he focuses on our capacity to respond to the most vulnerable among the diverse aged. Elizabeth Ann Kutza in Chapter 4 next explores the challenges in responding to diversity within the constraints of the U.S. political and economic systems.

In the fifth chapter, Harry R. Moody writes on the *opportunities* of a diverse aging society. His chapter on "the politics of entitlement" versus "the politics of productivity" argues that the elderly can contribute to society's prosperity through their productive involvement in it and thus dispel an image of selfishness and dependency.

Fernando Torres-Gil and Mimi Kmet in Chapter 6 address what may happen if we do *not* respond constructively and compassionately to the needs of the growing numbers of poor older persons, minority elderly, older women, and other disadvantaged elders.

The six chapters as a whole were designed to provide a new context in which to think about programs and services for the aged in the 1990s and beyond. The book was begun in anticipation of a

White House Conference on Aging, but it is also a resource guide for the next decade. We hope it will promote discussion of specific needs of our diverse and growing elderly population and serve as a framework in which specific categorical discussion can take place in a thoughtful and responsive manner.

CHAPTER ONE

Diversity: The Dramatic Reality

CYNTHIA TAEUBER

Diversity describes the elderly population of today and tomorrow in the United States. "The elderly"—commonly, the population 65 years and older—constitute a heterogeneous population. We cannot understand the complexities of their social and economic diversity from generalizations. For example, each age, gender, race, and ethnic group has distinctive characteristics. Rural elderly have different characteristics and needs than do urban elderly. The differences among the subgroups have implications for public policy.

Another effect on public policy is the sheer size and rate of growth of the older population. This is especially true among the "oldest old" (85 years and older) relative to other age groups. Along with the rapid growth of the older population in the United States, there have been changes in the proportion of young people.

The following section will show how changes in the levels of the basic demographic variables of fertility, mortality, and net migration have affected this country's age structure. After examining the growth of the elderly population and how it has occurred, we will describe their economic status, longevity, health characteristics, and social characteristics. Throughout, possible implications of the demographic changes will be examined.

Numerical Growth

Changes in age composition can have dramatic political, economic, and social effects on a nation. Seventy-five million children were born in the United States from 1946 to 1964. American society was adjusting to the size and needs of the baby-boom generation from the late 1940s through the 1970s. More recently, the baby boom has been the cause of ups and downs in the number of youth in college and the number entering the labor force. We face the reality of low fertility levels and the aging of the baby-boom generation after the year 2011, when the first wave of this group reaches age 65. After 2031, it is the size of the "oldest old" population that we will notice most, when the baby-boom generation begins to reach age 85. With such demographic facts staring us in the face, we are now more attentive to the implications of an aging society.

The aging of America is not new. In colonial times, half the population was under age 16. By 1987, fewer than one in four (22.9 percent) persons were younger than 16, and half the population was older than 32 years. By 2010, according to the Census Bureau's middle series projections, half the population will be 39 or older if levels of fertility, mortality, and net immigration all remain about the same as they are today. Likewise, by 2050, at least half will be 43 years old or older. If the levels of fertility, mortality, and net immigration are lower, half the population could be 50 or older by 2050.[1]

What is new is the rapid pace of aging. The number of persons aged 65 years and older has almost doubled since 1960, from nearly 17 million to a projected 32 million in 1990[2] (Table 1-1). According to the Census Bureau's middle series projections, the number of persons 65 years and older would more than double again by the middle of the next century to at least 69 million elderly. About one in eight Americans is elderly now, but as early as the year 2030 this ratio could be one in five.

OUR AGING WORLD

To set the aging of the United States in context, it is informative to look at the aging of the rest of the world. There are more

Table 1-1. Growth of the Older Population: 1900–2050

Year	Total (all ages)	55–64		65–74		75–79		80–84		85+		65+	
		Number	Percent	Number	Percent	Number	Percent	Number	Percent	Number	Percent	Number	Percent
ALL RACES*													
1900	75,995	4,003	5.3	2,187	2.9	520	0.7	252	0.3	122	0.2	3,081	4.1
1910	91,972	5,054	5.5	2,793	3.0	667	0.7	322	0.4	167	0.2	3,949	4.3
1920	105,711	6,532	6.2	3,464	3.3	856	0.8	403	0.4	210	0.2	4,933	4.7
1930	122,775	8,397	6.8	4,721	3.8	1,106	0.9	535	0.4	272	0.2	6,634	5.4
1940	131,669	10,572	8.0	6,376	4.8	1,504	1.1	774	0.6	365	0.3	9,019	6.8
1950	150,216	13,173	8.8	8,404	5.6	2,150	1.4	1,125	0.7	577	0.4	12,256	8.2
1960	179,323	15,572	8.7	10,997	6.1	3,054	1.7	1,580	0.9	929	0.5	16,560	9.2
1970	203,212	18,590	9.1	12,435	6.1	3,835	1.9	2,284	1.1	1,511	0.7	20,065	9.9
1980	226,546	21,703	9.6	15,581	6.9	4,794	2.1	2,935	1.3	2,240	1.0	25,550	11.3
1987	243,915	22,019	9.0	17,668	7.2	5,777	2.4	3,524	1.4	2,867	1.2	29,836	12.2
MIDDLE SERIES (middle fertility, mortality, and immigration assumptions)†													
ALL RACES													
1990	250,410	21,364	8.5	18,373	7.3	6,105	2.4	3,828	1.5	3,254	1.3	31,559	12.6
2000	268,266	24,158	9.0	18,243	6.8	7,282	2.7	4,735	1.8	4,622	1.7	34,882	13.0
2010	282,575	35,430	12.5	21,039	7.4	6,913	2.4	5,295	1.9	6,115	2.2	39,362	13.9
2020	294,364	41,087	14.0	30,973	10.5	8,981	3.1	5,462	1.9	6,651	2.3	52,067	17.7
2030	300,629	34,947	11.6	35,988	12.0	13,023	4.3	8,464	2.8	8,129	2.7	65,604	21.8
2040	301,807	35,537	11.8	30,808	10.2	14,260	4.7	10,790	3.6	12,251	4.1	68,109	22.6
2050	299,849	37,004	12.3	31,590	10.5	12,042	4.0	9,613	3.2	15,287	5.1	68,532	22.9
BLACK													
1990	31,148	2,156	6.9	1,608	5.2	489	1.6	265	0.9	251	0.8	2,613	8.4
2000	35,129	2,578	7.3	1,848	5.3	603	1.7	326	0.9	354	1.0	3,131	8.9
2010	38,833	3,995	10.3	2,277	5.9	687	1.8	419	1.1	478	1.2	3,861	9.9

*Figures for 1900 to 1950 exclude Alaska and Hawaii.

†For total population, assumes an ultimate total fertility rate of 1,800; life expectancy at birth in 2050 of 76.4 years for men and 83.3 years for women; and an ultimate net migration of 500,000 per year.

Table 1-1. Growth of the Older Population: 1900–2050 (cont.)

Year	Total (all ages)	55–64		65–74		75–79		80–84		85+		65+	
		Number	Percent	Number	Percent	Number	Percent	Number	Percent	Number	Percent	Number	Percent
BLACK (cont.)													
2020	42,128	5,221	12.4	3,580	8.5	906	2.2	501	1.2	600	1.4	5,587	13.3
2030	44,596	4,867	10.9	4,713	10.6	1,502	3.4	781	1.8	788	1.8	7,784	17.5
2040	46,239	5,224	11.3	4,459	9.6	1,853	4.0	1,179	2.5	1,287	2.8	8,778	19.0
2050	47,146	5,626	11.9	4,846	10.3	1,738	3.7	1,169	2.5	1,817	3.9	9,570	20.3
HISPANIC ORIGIN (may be of any race)—Series 14‡													
1990	19,887	1,183	5.9	707	3.6	197	1.0	127	0.6	95	0.5	1,126	5.7
2000	25,223	1,619	6.4	1,041	4.1	321	1.3	189	0.7	168	0.7	1,719	6.8
2010	30,795	2,704	8.8	1,432	4.7	445	1.4	312	1.0	288	0.9	2,477	8.0
2020	36,532	3,639	10.0	2,378	6.5	645	1.8	406	1.1	445	1.2	3,874	10.6
2030	41,899	3,809	9.1	3,181	7.6	1,076	2.6	674	1.6	647	1.5	5,578	13.3
2040	46,714	4,474	9.6	3,336	7.1	1,321	2.8	1,007	2.2	1,080	2.3	6,744	14.4
2050	50,790	5,402	10.6	3,930	7.7	1,393	2.7	1,071	2.1	1,514	3.0	7,908	15.6
HISPANIC ORIGIN (may be of any race)—Series 17 (High Net Immigration Series)§													
1990	21,854	1,207	5.5	713	3.3	199	0.9	130	0.6	96	0.4	1,138	5.2
2000	30,295	1,699	5.6	1,071	3.5	326	1.1	193	0.6	172	0.6	1,762	5.8
2010	39,526	2,900	7.3	1,510	3.8	462	1.2	321	0.8	294	0.7	2,587	6.5
2020	49,471	4,453	9.0	2,559	5.2	685	1.4	429	0.9	463	0.9	4,136	8.4
2030	59,445	5,262	8.9	3,901	6.6	1,169	2.0	718	1.2	686	1.2	6,474	10.9
2040	68,993	6,342	9.2	4,604	6.7	1,697	2.5	1,167	1.7	1,166	1.7	8,634	12.5
2050	77,676	7,896	10.2	5,559	7.2	1,935	2.5	1,455	1.9	1,826	2.4	10,775	13.9

‡Assumes constant immigration consistent with recent levels of legal immigration.
§Includes an allowance for undocumented immigration.
SOURCE: U.S. Bureau of the Census. 1980 Census of Population PC80-B1, General Population Characteristics, Tables 42 and 45; "Estimates of the Population of the United States by Age, Sex, and Race: 1980 to 1987," *Current Population Reports*, Series P-25, No. 1022. "Projections of the Population of the United States, by Age, Sex, and Race: 1988 to 2080," *Current Population Reports*, Series P-25, No. 1018: "Projections of the Hispanic Population: 1983 to 2080" (by G. Spencer), Series P-25, No. 995. Washington, D.C.: U.S. Government Printing Office, 1988.

than 290 million persons aged 65 and older in the world, and it is expected that there will be more than 400 million worldwide by the year 2000.[3] For the next twenty years, growth of the elderly population will be moderate for most nations. After 2010, however, the numbers of elderly will increase rapidly. The annual growth rate for the elderly will approach 4 percent (compared with an average annual rate of 2.4 percent from 1950 to 1980). Such growth is without historical precedent, and we expect it to continue far into the twenty-first century.

This trend is occurring in both developed and developing countries.[4] More than half (54 percent) of the world's elderly live in developing nations. These developing regions could be home to more than two-thirds (69 percent) of the world's elderly by the year 2025.

The level of fertility is a primary determinant of the age structure of a population. Population projections for China show that if the political desire to lower fertility to one child per married couple occurs nationwide, 40 percent of the population will be 65 years or older by the middle of the next century, compared with 5 percent in 1985. In the face of such a prospect, some Chinese planners have begun to reconsider their population goals.

Twenty-two nations, including China, had elderly populations of at least 2 million in 1985. Demographic projections indicate that there will be fifty such nations by 2025.

Sweden has the highest proportion of people aged 65 and older, with 17 percent in 1985, the same as the state of Florida. Sweden also has the highest proportion aged 80 and older—3.5 percent.

By 2025, the proportion of elderly of the populations of Sweden, Denmark, and West Germany could reach 22 percent; the rest of Europe and the United States will be close behind at about 20 percent.

Japan's population aged 65 and older would grow dramatically over the next twenty years. According to projections, the percentage of Japan's elderly could increase from 10 percent (about 12 million people) in 1985 to nearly 17 percent (nearly 22 million people) in 2005. This is a rapid rise in only two decades. Japan's post–World War II baby boom will assure continued expansion of the numbers of the elderly into the middle of the twenty-first century. Already the Japanese are reducing retirement benefits and making other adjustments to prepare for the economic and social results of a rapidly aging society.

Nine countries had more than one million octogenarians (80 years and older) in 1985. Octogenarians account for about one-fifth of the elderly population in developed countries, about one-tenth in developing countries. In many nations, demographers project this very old population to be the fastest growing portion of the elderly population through the middle of the next century.

Persons aged 80 and older numbered 6.4 million in the United States in 1987. They would number more than 14 million by 2025. China's 5.7 million octogenarians (1985) could increase to more than 25 million by 2025, and India's 3 million to more than 16 million over the same period.

The stunning growth of the oldest old has various health and economic implications for individuals, families, and governments throughout the world. The oldest old often have severe chronic health problems. This demands special attention because the nature and duration of their illnesses are likely to produce a need for prolonged care for many people. Developing nations already have diluted resources. They are the most limited in being able to provide preventive measures and, in future years, support services. The United States and other countries face enormous investments and payments to maintain current levels of services for the oldest old.

MORE RACIAL AND ETHNIC DIVERSITY IN THE UNITED STATES

We can expect to see more racial and ethnic diversity among our elders in the coming years. Of the total elderly population in the 1990 projection, 28.3 million are white; 2.6 million are black; 603,000 are other races; and 1.1 million are of Hispanic origin (but may be of any race) (see Figure 1-1).[5] According to the 1980 census, there were about 222,000 elderly Asians and Pacific Islanders and about 80,000 elderly American Indians, Eskimos, and Aleuts of 26 million total elderly.[6]

Of the 69 million elderly projected for 2050 (Figure 1-1), nearly 10 million would be black, 5 million would be persons of

Figure 1-1. Persons 65 Years and Over, by Age, Race, and Hispanic Origin: 1990 and 2050 (numbers in millions for population 65 and over)

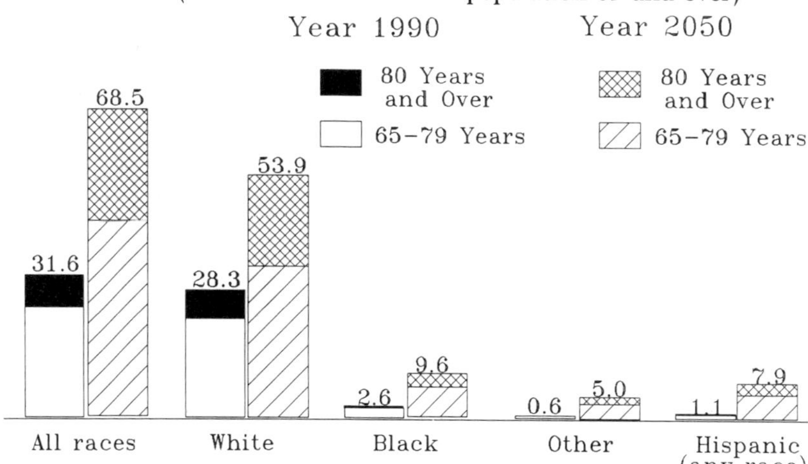

SOURCE: U.S. Bureau of the Census. "Projections of the Population of the United States, by Age, Sex, and Race: 1988 to 2080," *Current Population Reports*, Series P-25, No. 1018; "Projections of the Hispanic Population: 1983 to 2080," (by G. Spencer), Series P-25, No. 995. Washington, D.C.: U.S. Government Printing Office, 1988. Middle series projections.

races other than white or black, and 8 million would be Hispanic.[7] If mortality rates improve, the numbers for all groups will be even higher.

Although races other than white now constitute about one in ten of the elderly, by 2050, that proportion may increase to two in ten (Figure 1-2).[8] Using middle series projections for 1990 and 2050, elderly blacks could increase their proportion of the total elderly population from 8 to 14 percent (Figure 1-3), races other than white or black could increase from 2 to 7 percent (Figure 1-4), and Hispanics from less than 4 percent to nearly 12 percent (Figure 1-5).

The white population has a higher proportion of elderly than other racial groups or Hispanics (Figure 1-6). In the 1990 projections, nearly 14 percent of the white population will be elderly compared with 8 percent of the black population and almost 6 percent of the Hispanic population. In 1980, 6 percent of Asians and Pacific Islanders were elderly compared with 5 percent of American Indians, Eskimos, and Aleuts. By 2030 (when the baby-boom generation is 65 to 85 years old), about 18 percent of black Americans and 13 percent of Hispanics could be 65 or older. A much larger

Figure 1-2. Elderly White Population as a Percentage of Total Elderly Population: 1990 to 2080 (population 65 Years and Over)

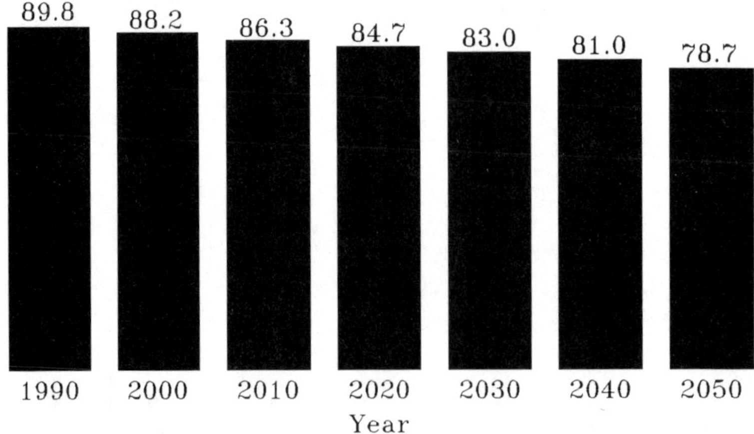

SOURCE: U.S. Bureau of the Census. "Projections of the Population of the United States, by Age, Sex, and Race: 1988 to 2080," *Current Population Reports,* Series P-25, No. 1018. Washington, D.C.: U.S. Government Printing Office, 1988. Middle series projections.

Figure 1-3. Elderly Black Population as a Percentage of Total Elderly Population: 1990 to 2080 (population 65 Years and Over)

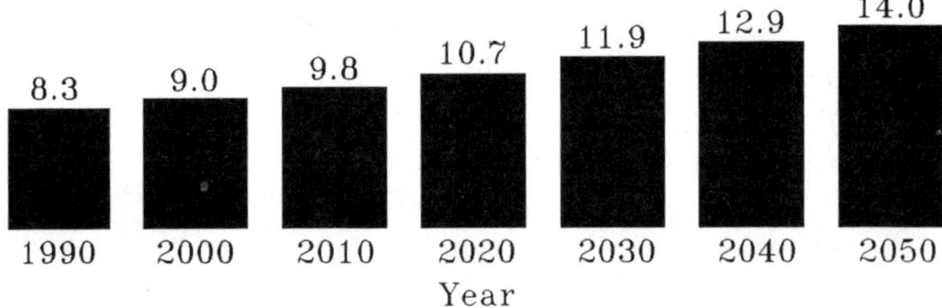

SOURCE: U.S. Bureau of the Census. "Projections of the Population of the United States, by Age, Sex, and Race: 1988 to 2080," *Current Population Reports,* Series P-25, No. 1018. Washington, D.C.: U.S. Government Printing Office, 1988. Middle series projections.

proportion of the white population, 23 percent, may be elderly. The proportions will remain roughly the same for whites through 2050 but will increase slowly for other groups.

POPULATION PROJECTIONS: 1990 TO 2010

The primary reason for the numerical growth of the older population is the growth in the number of births in past years. Increases in longevity are a secondary cause of growth except among the oldest old. The improved chance of survival to the oldest ages is the most important factor in the growth of the oldest old population.[9]

Past immigration of relatively young Hispanic persons is an additional major factor in the eventual rapid growth of the elderly population.

After peaking at 3.1 million in 1921, the annual number of births declined to less than 2.5 million during the early 1930s and did not rise permanently above 3 million until 1946. As a result, we can expect to see sustained but undramatic growth of the total elderly population until about 2010. Planners call this period a "window of opportunity," a time to plan and prepare for the aging of the baby-boom generation.

POPULATION PROJECTIONS: 2010 TO 2030

Growth of the older population will be more dramatic after 2010 with the aging of the baby-boom generation. This cohort represents one-third of the American population now. Over the two decades from 2010 to 2030, when this group is aged 64 to 84, the elderly population may well grow eleven times faster than the total population, depending on what happens to rates of fertility, mortality, and immigration.[10]

POPULATION PROJECTIONS: 2030 TO 2050

The final phase of the gerontological explosion will begin in 2030. It will continue through the middle of the twenty-first century when the surviving members of the baby-boom generation begin to

Figure 1-4. Elderly Other Races Population as a Percentage of Total Elderly Population: 1990 to 2080 (population 65 years and over; "other races" are primarily Asians, Pacific Islanders, and American Indians)

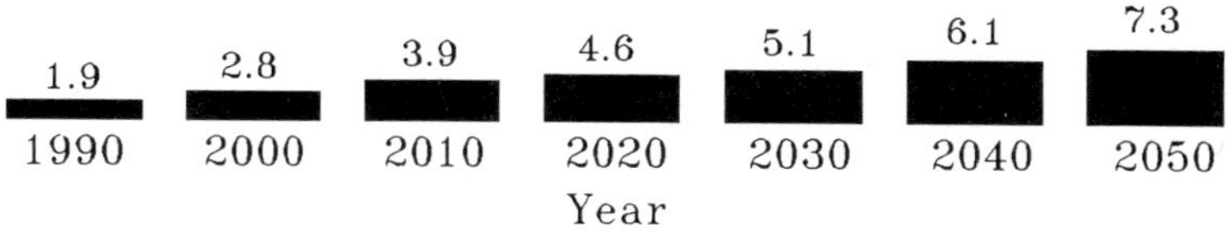

1.9	2.8	3.9	4.6	5.1	6.1	7.3
1990	2000	2010	2020	2030	2040	2050

Year

SOURCE: U.S. Bureau of the Census. "Projections of the Population of the United States, by Age, Sex, and Race: 1988 to 2080," *Current Population Reports*, Series P-25, No. 1018. Washington, D.C.: U.S. Government Printing Office, 1988. Middle series projections.

Figure 1-5. Elderly Hispanic Population as a Percentage of Total Elderly Population: 1990 to 2080 (population 65 years and over; Hispanics may be of any race)

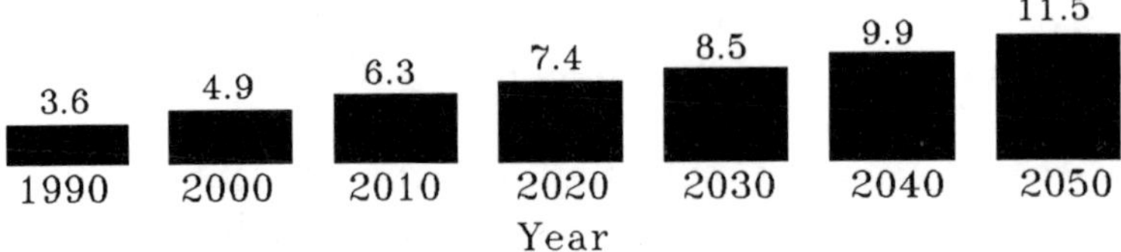

SOURCE: U.S. Bureau of the Census. "Projections of the Population of the United States, by Age, Sex, and Race: 1988 to 2080," *Current Population Reports,* Series P-25, No. 1018; "Projections of the Hispanic Population: 1983 to 2080" (by G. Spencer), Series P-25, No. 995. Washington, D.C.: U.S. Government Printing Office, 1988. Middle series projections.

Figure 1-6. Percentage of the Population 65 Years and Over: 1990 and 2050

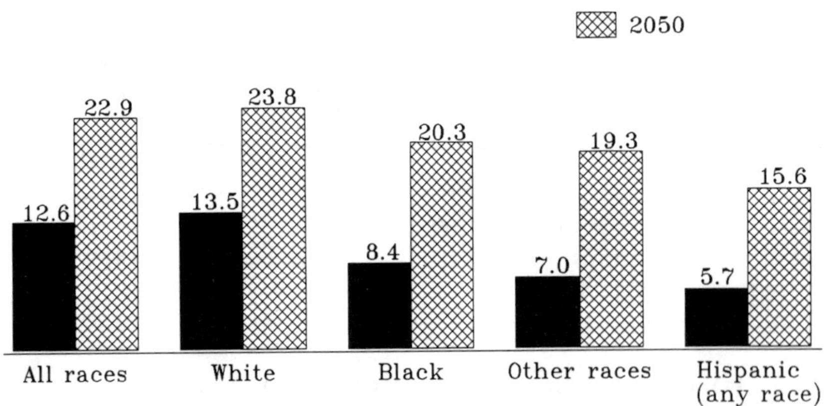

SOURCE: U.S. Bureau of the Census. "Projections of the Population of the United States, by Age, Sex, and Race: 1988 to 2080," *Current Population Reports,* Series P-25, No. 1018; "Projections of the Hispanic Population: 1983 to 2080" (by G. Spencer), Series P-25, No. 995. Washington, D.C.: U.S. Government Printing Office, 1988. Middle series projections.

reach age eighty-five. By 2040, according to middle series projections, we will have more people aged 65 and older (68.1 million) than we have persons younger than twenty years of age (67.7 million). The size and proportion of the total population 65 years and older will barely change for the two decades from 2030 to 2050. This is because the cohorts born after the baby boom, from 1965 to 1984, will be aged 65 to 84 years in 2050. That age group could decrease from 57 million in 2030 to 54 million in 2050. The significant growth will be among the oldest old. The population aged 85 years and older could nearly double, from 8 million to 15 million, as the baby-boom cohort reaches the oldest ages.

The aging of the aged, the "great-grandma boom," will be upon us. Today, one in forty Americans are aged 80 or older; by 2050, one in twelve persons could be 80 years or older. If life expectancy improves more rapidly than the Census Bureau's middle series projections assume, the size and proportion of the elderly population would be even larger than the numbers shown here.

As indicated by the numbers above, the elderly population is itself "aging." By that we mean that a larger proportion of those aged 65 and older are in the oldest ages. By 1990, we expect that about one-fifth of elderly blacks and of elderly Hispanics will be 80 years or older. By 2050, this proportion could increase to almost one-third. The proportions are somewhat higher for whites (Figure 1-7).

MORE OLDER WOMEN THAN OLDER MEN

Elderly women outnumber men three to two, a change from 1930 when they were about equal in number. In 1987, there were about 5.6 million more elderly women than elderly men. The differences between the number of men and women grow with advancing age. At ages 65 to 69, women outnumber men five to four; for those 85 years and older, women outnumber men five to two.

The death of a husband often marks the point of economic reversals for the surviving wife. In the future, we expect a delay in this problem as more men live to older ages. We also expect more women to have their own pensions. By the middle of the next century, we expect to see about three elderly men to four elderly women among both whites and blacks. Even among the oldest old, by 2050 we may see improvement to a ratio of one man 85 years and older to two women that age. However, because women are more likely than men to survive to the oldest ages, the health, social, and economic problems of the oldest old are primarily the problems of women. This fact has implications for both personal decisions and government policy.

Figure 1-7. Percentage of the Elderly (65+) Population Aged 80 or Older: 1990 and 2050

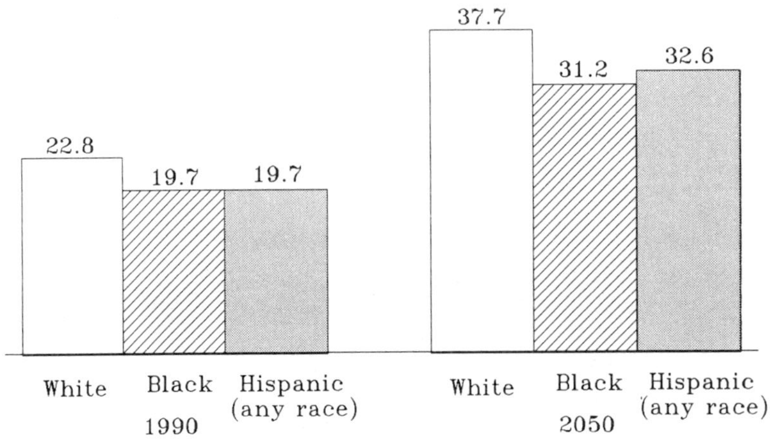

SOURCE: U.S. Bureau of the Census. "Projections of the Population of the United States, by Age, Sex, and Race: 1988 to 2080," *Current Population Reports,* Series P-25, No. 1018; "Projections of the Hispanic Population: 1983 to 2080" (by G. Spencer), Series P-25, No. 995. Washington, D.C.: U.S. Government Printing Office, 1988. Middle series projections.

FAMILIAL SUPPORT RATIOS

It is increasingly likely that more and more people in their fifties and sixties will have surviving parents. The four-generation family will become common. Children will know their grandparents and even their great-grandparents, especially their great-grandmothers. And more people will face the concern and expense of caring for their very old, frail parents since so many people now live long enough to face multiple, chronic illnesses. A relatively large proportion of the baby-boom generation is childless (37 percent).[11] They may face institutionalization at earlier ages than those with children.

An approximate idea of things to come can be seen in the "familial dependency ratios" suggested by demographer Siegel[12] (Table 1-2). These ratios reflect the way the age composition of the population affects the ratio of older persons to adults who could be their children. The ratios are also indicators of the extent of the need for family support over time. Siegel defines the ratio for one elderly generation as the ratio of persons aged 65 to 79 to persons aged 45 to 49. From 1990 to 2010, the baby-boom generation will swell the size of the group aged 45 to 49. The ratio for one elderly generation

Table 1-2. Familial Dependency Ratios: 1990 to 2050

Generations/Race	1990	2010	2030	2050
ONE ELDERLY GENERATION*				
Total	176	130	254	243
White	182	134	266	249
Black	146	109	228	237
Other races	106	116	173	203
Hispanic (any race)	97	96	169	170
TWO ELDERLY GENERATIONS†				
Total	32	50	43	88
White	33	53	45	95
Black	27	36	30	67
Other races	18	31	43	68
Hispanic (any race)	23	35	38	69

* $\frac{\text{Population aged 65–79}}{\text{Population aged 45–49}} \times 100$ † $\frac{\text{Population 85+ years}}{\text{Population aged 65–69}} \times 100$

SOURCE: U.S. Bureau of the Census.

will decrease somewhat, from 176 to 130. Hence, all else remaining equal, the overall level of support of the "young old" would also decrease. From 2010 to 2030, however, the baby-boom generation will be aged 65 to 85. In those 20 years, the ratio will double for blacks and whites and increase considerably for other race groups and Hispanics. The average age for the onset of serious, chronic illnesses differs among other races and Hispanic groups. Thus, the "one elderly generation" ratio is probably more significant to minority families than to white families.

Siegel defines the ratio for two elderly generations (Table 1-2) as the ratio of persons aged 65 to 69 to persons aged 85 years and older. The ratio is highest for whites, but changes in this ratio are meaningful to every race and ethnic group. The oldest old are the most likely to have pressing needs for economic and physical support. The need for help is likely to come at the very time when the adult children of the frail oldest old have reached the age of retirement. Some bear health limitations of their own. The "two elderly generation ratio" will increase steadily from 1990 to 2010. It will decrease somewhat from 2010 to 2030 because the group aged 65 to 69 will be relatively large, a result of the baby boom. The ratio will double for whites and blacks from 2030 to 2050[13] when the baby-boom generation reaches the oldest old ages.

There is no historical precedent for the experience of most middle-aged and young-old persons having living parents. Menken has estimated that one in three 50-year-old women had living mothers in 1940, and that by 1980, that proportion had already doubled to two in three.[14]

Families, especially adult daughters and daughters-in-law, provide 80 to 90 percent of personal care and help with household tasks, transportation, and shopping for the elderly. Elaine Brody conservatively estimates that more than 5 million adult children provide parent care.[15] The nature of the care is much more demanding and the duration is longer than in the "good ol' days." Life expectancy of the disabled, the mentally retarded, and the chronically ill has increased. As medical technology provides more ways to save lives, we can expect to see the duration of chronic illness increase even more. As a result, older people will need help longer. Women particularly may have to leave the work force or work part-time to care for frail parents at just the time when they themselves are working to be sure they receive retirement benefits for their own old age. As a result of delayed childbearing, many women will have responsibility for college-age children and frail parents, all while trying to hold a job or adjust to their own retirement, widowhood, or reduced income.

SOCIETAL SUPPORT RATIOS

With changes in the balance of the numbers and proportions in broad age groups, public policy issues often arise. We can show the broad changes in our age structure by "societal support ratios." These are ratios of the number of young people (younger than age 20), the elderly (65 years and older), and the aged (75 years and older) per one hundred persons aged 20 to 64 years, the principal ages for participation in the labor force.

From 1990 to 2050, the total support ratio (youth plus elderly in relation to the working-age population) will not change much for race groups other than whites (68.7 to 83.5) and will decrease somewhat for Hispanics (81.1 to 74.5). There will be, however, a profound shift in the composition of the total support ratio (SR) as the elderly population increases and the young population decreases (Figure 1-8). Within the white population, the youth SR will decrease somewhat but the elderly SR will nearly double and will be much higher than for the other groups. For the other groups, the decrease in the youth SR is as notable as the increase in the elderly SR.

The most significant point about the elderly SR is that the population 75 years and older is an increasingly larger proportion (Figure 1-9). The "aged" (75 and older) are more likely than the "young old" (65 to 74 years) to have major health and disability limitations and reduced economic resources. For each group, those aged 65 to 74 form the largest proportion of the elderly SR in 1990. By 2050, however, the 75 and older population could be about half of the elderly SR (more than half for whites).

Of course, not all youth and elderly require support, nor do all working-age persons actually work or provide support. The ratios are useful as indicators of potential change in the levels of economic and physical support needed. They are indicators of the periods when we can expect the particular age distribution of the country to affect the need for distinct types of social services, housing, and consumer products. Some argue that the stability of the total SR over time is more pertinent to policymakers than the changes in the composition of the support ratio. Others argue that it is more

Figure 1-8. Ratios of Youth and Elderly to Other Adults, by Race and Hispanic Origin: 1990 and 2050 (number of persons of given age per 100 persons aged 20–64)

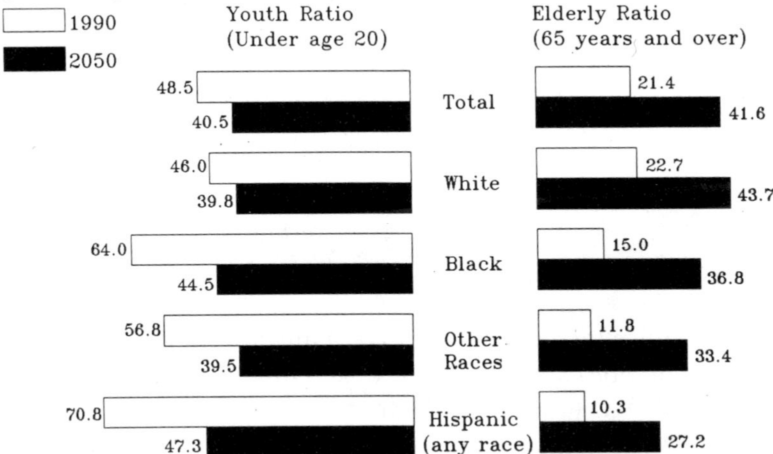

SOURCE: U.S. Bureau of the Census. "Projections of the Population of the United States, by Age, Sex, and Race: 1988 to 2080," *Current Population Reports*, Series P-25, No. 1018; "Projections of the Hispanic Population: 1983 to 2080" (by G. Spencer), Series P-25, No. 995. Washington, D.C.: U.S. Government Printing Office, 1988. Middle series projections.

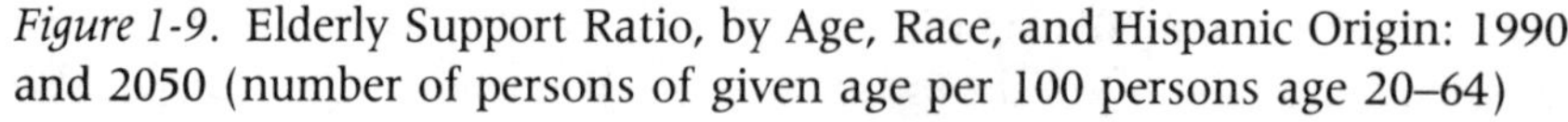

Figure 1-9. Elderly Support Ratio, by Age, Race, and Hispanic Origin: 1990 and 2050 (number of persons of given age per 100 persons age 20–64)

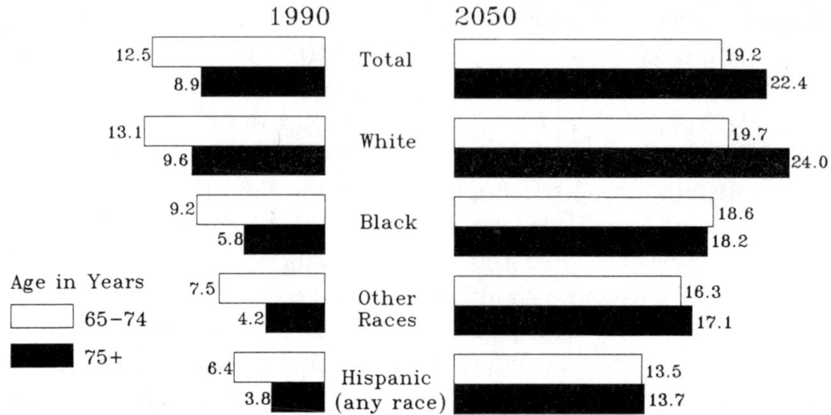

SOURCE: U.S. Bureau of the Census. "Projections of the Population of the United States, by Age, Sex, and Race: 1988 to 2080," *Current Population Reports,* Series P-25, No. 1018; "Projections of the Hispanic Population: 1983 to 2080" (by G. Spencer), Series P-25, No. 995. Washington, D.C., U.S. Government Printing Office, 1988. Middle series projections.

important to know the balance of old versus young because the relative costs of supporting the young are probably less than those of supporting the elderly[16] (especially as the elderly population itself ages). Further, the costs of young people are borne by families more than by government programs (with the major exception of education). Certainly, much depends on the health and economic resources of the aged population of the future.

Longevity and Health Characteristics

LONGEVITY AND CAUSES OF DEATH

Impressive increases in life expectancy add to the growth of the older population. Since 1970, average remaining life expectancy at 65 years of age has increased from 1.0 to 1.7 years, but the increase has varied among race-sex groups.[17] The most dramatic reductions in mortality have occurred among women and among the oldest old. This is primarily because of reductions in mortality rates from major cardiovascular diseases.[18]

Life expectancy at birth was about 75 years for all races in 1986. In the Census Bureau's middle series projections, it is expected to continue upward but at a slower rate than over the last two decades. Women have a higher life expectancy than men; there are also racial differences. In 1986, life expectancy was nearly 79 years for white women, 74 years for black women, 72 years for white men, and 65 years for black men. In 1900, by contrast, life expectancy at birth was about 49 years for white women and 47 years for white men; for races other than white, life expectancy was 34 years for women and 33 years for men. At that time, one in five white children and one in three children of races other than white died before their fifth birthday. Now, only 1 to 3 percent (depending on sex and race) of such young children die.

Among men, average remaining life expectancy from 1979 to 1981 was higher for whites until age 70 to 71. After that age, men of races other than white could expect to live as long or longer than white men. Among women, the statistical crossover occurred after age 75 when women of races other than white recorded higher life expectancy.[19] There is controversy whether the statistical crossover is real or an artifact of poor data on blacks at the older ages. Many statisticians believe that for those who have survived to age 85, black women have longer life expectancies than do white or black men.[20]

Under the middle mortality assumption for 2050, blacks and whites would have similar life expectancies, although the gender gap is projected to remain: white and black women, 84 years and 82 years, respectively; white and black men, 77 years and 75 years, respectively.[21]

Death before the mid-sixties is relatively unusual, especially for whites and Hispanics. According to decennial life tables for 1979 to 1981, 80 percent of whites and Hispanics would survive to age 65, but only 66 percent of blacks and 71 percent of American Indians would survive to that age.[22]

Based on the mortality experience of 1986, black men aged 65 can expect to live nearly fourteen additional years, as compared with almost seventeen years for 65-year-old black women, fifteen years for white males, and nineteen years for white females. By 2050, average remaining life expectancy of 65-year-old women would be 22 years, compared with seventeen years for men that age.

There were about 2 million deaths in the United States in 1985. Nearly 1.1 million persons aged 65 to 84 and 0.4 million persons aged 85 and older died. After 2010, when the baby-boom generation begins to reach age 65, demographers project the number of deaths to rise quickly (3.5 million in 2030). By 2030, there would be more deaths than births every year under the middle series projections. Death rates are higher for men than for women in every age group 55 years and older. Young-old men, in particular, have experienced reduced mortality since the 1970s. In 1970, among men aged 55 to 64, there were about twenty-two white male deaths and about thirty-three black male deaths per 1,000 population. By 1984, the deaths had decreased to sixteen and twenty-seven per 1,000 population, respectively. The rates for women that age were much lower (in 1984, per 1,000 population, there were fewer than nine deaths for white women and about fifteen for black women). Among white women, the most significant proportionate decrease in death rates from 1970 to 1984 was among older women, aged 75 to 84 years (23.3 percent). For black women, the greatest gains were among young-old women aged 55 to 74 (about 25 percent). White women aged 85 years and older had the largest absolute decrease in rates since 1970, with about twenty-four fewer deaths per 1,000 population. Most of the reductions in death rates occurred before 1979.[23]

In the future, analysts expect the proportion of deaths at older ages to continue to increase. Most striking is the projected increase in the proportion of deaths at age 85 and older. While 20 percent of all deaths now occur at such old ages, this percentage would reach 30 percent by 2010 and at least 43 percent after 2050.[24]

Three of four elderly die from heart disease, cancer, or stroke. Influenza and pneumonia are also important causes of death after age 85.[25] Heart disease is the leading cause of death within the elderly population and is the cause of death for about four in ten of the young old and about half of the oldest old (85 and older).

Of those aged 55 to 74 years, black men have the highest rates of death from both heart disease (Figure 1-10) and cancer (Figure 1-11), followed by white men. For cerebrovascular diseases, blacks have significantly higher death rates than whites of both sexes until the oldest ages (Figure 1-12).

Even though heart disease is the major killer of the elderly, death rates from ischemic heart disease have decreased significantly for all older age groups over the last few decades as have death rates

Figure 1-10. Death Rates for Diseases of the Heart for Persons 55 Years and Over, by Age, Sex, and Race: 1984 (number of deaths per 100,000 resident population)

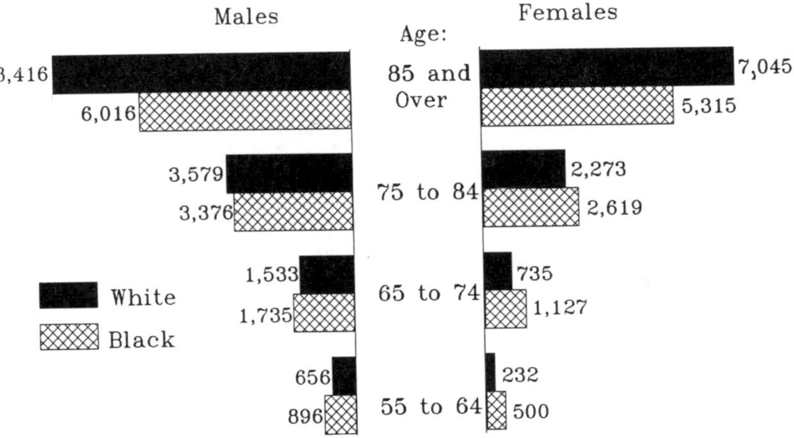

SOURCE: Havlik, R., B. Liu, M. Kovar, et al. National Center for Health Statistics, "Health Statistics on Older Persons, United States: 1986," *Vital and Health Statistics,* Series 3, No. 25, DHHS Pub. No. (PHS)87-1409. Washington, D.C.: U.S. Government Printing Office, June 1987, Table 4, p. 9.

Figure 1-11. Death Rates for Malignant Neoplasms for Persons 55 Years and Over, by Age, Sex, and Race: 1984 (number of deaths per 100,000 resident population; includes neoplasms of lymphatic and hematopoietic tissues)

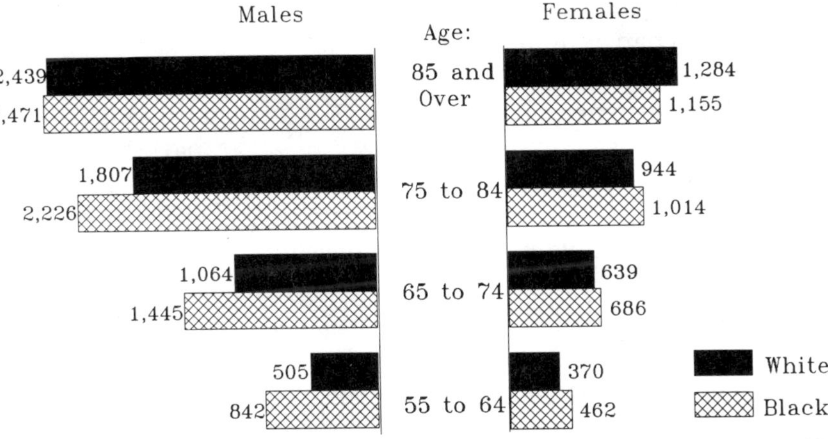

SOURCE: Havlik, R., B. Liu, M. Kovar, et al. National Center for Health Statistics, "Health Statistics on Older Persons, United States: 1986," *Vital and Health Statistics,* Series 3, No. 25, DHHS Pub. No. (PHS)87-1409. Washington, D.C.: U.S. Government Printing Office, June 1987, Table 7, p. 12.

Figure 1-12. Death Rates for Cerebrovascular Diseases for Persons 55 Years and Over, by Age, Sex, and Race: 1984 (number of deaths per 100,000 resident population)

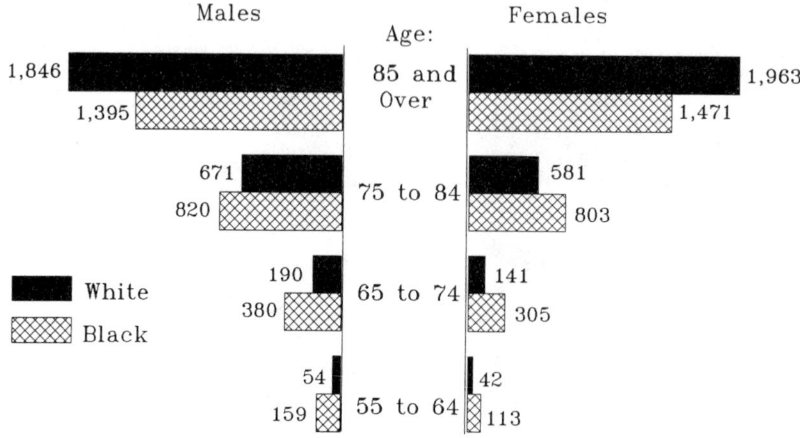

SOURCE: Havlik, R., B. Liu, M. Kovar, et al. National Center for Health Statistics, "Health Statistics on Older Persons, United States: 1986," *Vital and Health Statistics,* Series 3, No. 25, DHHS Pub. No. (PHS)87-1409. Washington, D.C: U.S. Government Printing Office, June 1987, Table 6, p. 11.

from cerebrovascular diseases. Death rates from cancer, however, have been increasing since 1968.[26]

The changes in life expectancy, and the change from a large proportion of deaths occurring in early ages to the oldest ages, obviously have ponderous implications for financing a long life even if medical science somehow manages to make old age perfectly healthy. And, as life expectancy continues to increase, issues about the quality of life of older people face us. The financial soundness of retirement plans could be critical to an ever-larger proportion of the population.[27] We can expect to see more chronic illness, disability, and dependency.

HEALTH AND DISABILITY STATUS

Many people assume that if mortality rates have decreased, health among the elderly must have improved. They also hold the contradictory image of the elderly as having frail health. Poor health is not as prevalent as many assume, especially among the young old.

In 1983 to 1984, only about one in nine persons aged 65 to 74 reported that chronic illness prevented them from carrying out their usual activities. Of those elderly living in households, two of three whites reported that their health was good or excellent compared with about half of elderly blacks.[28]

But, more people live to the oldest ages, and they may live their increased years with multiple illnesses and disabilities. For example, physicians save the lives of many people who used to die of heart attacks but these people face the remainder of their years with chronic, limiting illness.[29] Among those eighty-five years and older, almost one in four lives in an institution because of serious health problems. Of those living in households, one in five is unable to carry on a major activity and two in five have a condition that limits their activities.[30]

With increasing age, the rates of hearing and visual impairments increase rapidly. Half of the oldest old population (noninstitutionalized) had problems with hearing. More than half of the 65-and-older population living in households reported that they had arthritis, and the incidence was especially high among women and blacks (for example, nearly two in three elderly black women report that they suffer from arthritis). The second most frequently reported chronic condition is hypertension, a disease that is especially prevalent among black women.[31]

The health of the oldest population, which clearly declines with increasing age, suggests that a larger number will seek long-term care as part of the continuum from independent living, to assisted living at home, to institutional care. The number requiring services for nonfatal conditions can be expected to increase unless there are medical revolutions on several fronts.

Men tend to develop fatal diseases, whereas women are more likely to have chronic disabling diseases. This has significance for differences in the nature and duration of long-term care for men and women. This difference is also significant in the discussion by ethicist Callahan on setting medical goals in an aging society.[32] Restrictions to access to medical care would directly affect men the most since they are more likely to require medical interventions that affect length of life rather than quality of life. Restrictions to medical care for otherwise fatal diseases would more indirectly affect women who lose the companionship and economic support of their husbands.

Economic Characteristics

WORK AND RETIREMENT

Labor Force Participation. More and more people are retiring early—that is, before the age when they can receive full retirement benefits. For example, older men are less likely to be in the labor force today than they were thirty years ago. In 1950, two-thirds (68.6 percent) of men aged 55 and older, and nearly half (45.8 percent) of men aged 65 and older, were in the labor force. In 1988, about two in five men aged 55 and older (39.9 percent), and about one in six elderly men (16.5 percent) were in the labor force. Women have become a larger share of the older work force, and analysts anticipate that that trend will continue. The female share of the older (55 and older) work force nearly doubled from 1950 to 1988. In 1988, the 6.3 million women aged 55 and older in the civilian labor force accounted for four in ten of all older workers.[33] Lower pensions, savings, and Social Security are all spread over a longer period than in the past for many retirees as a result of early retirement and increased life expectancy.

Labor force participation among men aged 55 to 59 years has also shown record declines in the last twenty years. In 1967, 90.1 percent of men that age were in the labor force compared with 79.3 percent in 1988. In 1967, 48.4 percent of women aged 55 to 59 worked in the paid labor market, compared with 53.3 percent in 1988.[34–37]

For women aged 65 years and older, there has been little change in labor force participation rates from 1957 to 1988 (10.5 percent in 1957; 7.9 percent in 1988).[38] As they age, elderly women who work often reduce the length of their work week and the number of weeks they work in a year. In 1986, more than half of women, aged 55 to 61 worked full time and year round compared with only one-fourth of women aged 65 and older who worked such schedules.

Women aged 50 years and older grew up in an age when society did not encourage or expect women to work outside the home. They have been less likely to be in the labor force at every age than is true of younger cohorts. For example, seven of ten women

(73.1 percent) in their thirties were in the labor force in 1988, double the proportion of three decades earlier.[39, 40] As a result of the greater likelihood of working, young and middle-aged women are increasingly likely to have been in the labor force long enough to have savings, pensions, and Social Security in their own names, which could make a significant difference in their economic status as they age.

When compared with the distribution of occupations of all workers, fewer of America's 3 million elderly workers are in blue-collar occupations and more and more are in service occupations. The proportion of elderly in white-collar occupations is about the same as in the total labor force.[41]

Most older (and younger) women still work in occupations traditionally held predominantly by women.[42, 43] In 1987, two in three working women 55 years and older held jobs in retail sales, administrative support (includes clerical), and services. Elderly women are particularly overrepresented in sales and service (especially private household) jobs; these are jobs that are more amenable to part-time work, are less likely to have provided pension coverage when the women were younger, and are less physically demanding for those with health limitations.[44]

As noted by Rones and Herz, "Older women are probably at the greatest disadvantage in the labor market; on average, they have less experience than men and less education than both men and younger women."[45] In 1987, four in ten women aged fifty-five or older had not completed high school (same as older men) compared with only one in ten women aged 25 to 34. Two-thirds of older black women had less than a high school education. Only 9 percent of older women had completed four or more years of college compared with 16 percent of older men and 22 percent of women aged 25 to 34.[46]

White, black, and Hispanic women 55 years and older are nearly as likely to be in the labor force (respectively, 21.5, 24.7, and 22.2 percent in 1987), but black and Hispanic women are more concentrated in relatively few low-paying occupations.[47] In 1987, for example, about half (49.3 percent) of employed black women 55 to 64 years old and nearly one-third (31.1 percent) of Hispanic women that age worked in a service occupation, compared with one in six (15.9 percent) white women.[48] Older black women, compared with older white women, are less likely to receive a pension, to have completed high school, to own their homes or other valuable assets, or to be married; hence, they have fewer resources for retirement.[49] It is unlikely that the occupational differences between older black and white women will be as pronounced in the future as now.[50]

More than half of all workers are in white-collar occupations. In the future, a greater proportion of elderly will have pensions, and that may reduce their desire to work. In 1983, four in five pension plans had no minimum retirement age or provided full benefits at age 62; more than one in three permitted retirement as early as age 55 with thirty years of service.[51] In short, more people can afford to retire early. The elderly who want or need to work will compete with younger people and women of all ages, especially for part-time work. Many predict future labor shortages because of the "baby bust," and this may lessen the competition faced by the elderly.

Part-time Employment. Most older persons reject employment, including part-time employment, although in surveys they express a preference for phased retirement.[52, 53] Well-paid part-time work is rare for any age group, and usually there are few fringe benefits. Elderly persons represented about 7 percent of all persons in nonagricultural industries on part-time schedules in 1988. Nevertheless, an increasing proportion of those elderly who remain in the labor force work part-time. Of elderly persons who worked in 1988 in nonagricultural industries, 46 percent of the men and 60 percent of the women worked on part-time schedules compared with 1960 when only 30 percent of the men and 44 percent of the women worked part-time.[54–56]

Unemployment and Other Labor Market Problems. Older workers may not be as protected from job loss as is often assumed. About 490,000 persons aged 55 years and older were unemployed in 1987 (of a total unemployment count of 7.4 million); fewer than 80,000 were aged 65 years and older.[57] Data limitations make it difficult to say much about job loss and employment opportunities among older people. The Rones and Herz report shows that official unemployment rates for the older population are now lower than those of the younger population (even if we include discouraged workers who stopped actively looking for work). Nevertheless, most unemployed workers aged 55 to 64 were (1) laid off or permanently separated from their jobs, (2) looking for full-time work, and (3) did not have income adequate to support themselves if they left the labor force (the three groups are not necessarily composed of the same people). While many older unemployed workers have Social Security or pension income, many do not. Economic circumstances may hinder job hunting. For example, of unemployed men aged 62 to 64 years in 1987, 45 percent had neither pension nor Social Security income and 40 percent had only Social Security.[58]

Older workers, especially women, tend to be more concentrated in declining industries (for example, manufacturing, textiles), which puts them at a relatively higher risk for losing their jobs. Women, and especially men, often suffer a significant decline in earnings if they find new employment. In 1986, one-fifth (18.7 percent) of all displaced workers (20 years and older) were 55 or older. Among these older displaced workers, about two-thirds reported losing their jobs because of plant closings. Displacement among older workers has a permanent negative economic effect. Further, the incidence and severity of labor market problems of older workers increase considerably in recessions.[59]

Before the 1970s, the jobless rate for older men was usually higher than for men aged 25 to 54. Since then, the situation has reversed and now favors older men, probably because of options not available to younger workers. Such options include (1) improvements in Social Security and private pension plans that have made retirement a viable alternative to employment and (2) the increased use of early retirement inducements. Retirees are less likely to re-enter the labor force once they have retired than they were in the late 1960s and the early 1970s.[60]

There is little data on unemployment and other labor market problems of older racial and ethnic minorities. This is primarily because surveys of the labor force are too small to measure the job market status of small population groups. As noted in a 1989 report of the secretary of labor:

> There is no question that older blacks and other minorities are far more likely than whites to experience labor market problems. Limited available data suggest that older minority workers, like those of all ages, have higher rates of unemployment and

> discouragement and lower earnings than do older whites. These lifetime differences in employment and earnings generally mean fewer resources at retirement age. As a result, some older workers must maintain attachment to the job market long after those with greater financial resources might have retired.[61]

Additionally, the 1985 National Commission for Employment Policy found that older blacks were four times and older Hispanics were three times as likely as older whites to experience labor market problems.[62]

INCOME AND ASSETS

The income level of the older population is, in general, at a considerably lower level after retirement and is less secure than that of the younger population. Once the elderly spend their assets, they are less likely to replace them. The overall position of "the elderly" has improved significantly since the 1970s. There is evidence that for the total elderly population, assets increase with age up until the early eighties. Homes are the major asset of most elderly persons.[63]

For those older persons with retirement income indexed to increase with inflation, their income is affected less than that of the younger population. Using constant 1987 dollars, the median income of the population 65 and older has more than doubled since 1957 (from $5,740 to $11,850 for elderly men; and from $2,990 to $6,730 for elderly women).[64]

But it is misleading to talk about the total "elderly" population. Income differences are significant for population subgroups defined by characteristics such as age, sex, race, ethnicity, living arrangement, educational attainment, former occupational status, and work history. Rural elderly and the elderly in southern states had the lowest median incomes in 1980 and the highest proportion of poor elderly. Characteristics such as older average age, lower educational attainment, and lower occupational status explain the differences better than place of residence.[65, 66]

The income of elderly women, especially widows living alone, tends to be considerably lower than that of elderly men. Incomes greater than $20,000 are more likely among men aged 55 to

64 and among married-couple families. Where the householder was 55 to 64 in 1988, three of four (77 percent) married-couple families had incomes of $20,000 or more, compared with more than one-third (39 percent) of men and about one-fourth (23 percent) of women that age who were "unrelated individuals" (most of whom were widows living alone). About half (53 percent) of married-couple families with a householder aged 65 or older had incomes greater than $20,000 annually.[67]

Among elderly subgroups, white men had much higher incomes on average than other groups. In 1979, median incomes for persons 65 years and older ranged from $2,800 for black women to $7,400 for white men (Figure 1-13).

Social Security benefits are the single largest source of money income for the retired and the single source on which the largest proportion is most dependent. Since the 1960s, there has been a marked increase in reliance on Social Security and a decline in the importance of earnings although earnings make a great difference in the economic position of older persons. In 1940, less than 1 percent of the elderly received Social Security benefits and 22

Figure 1-13. Median Income in 1979 of Persons 65 and Over: 1980 (dollars in thousands)

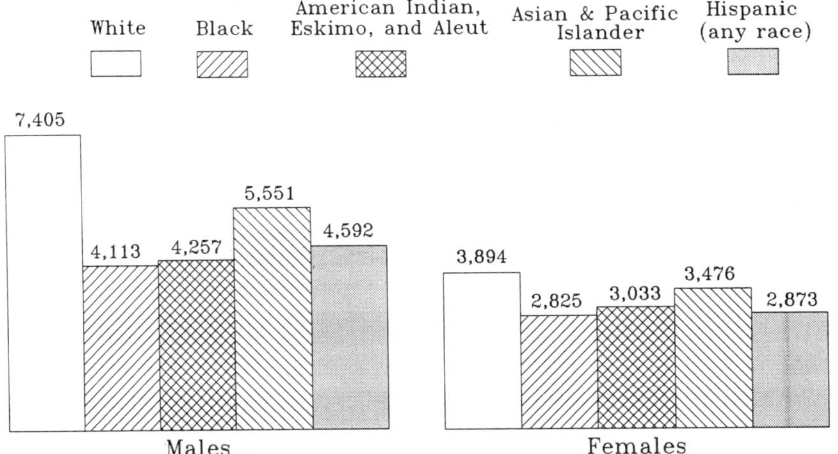

SOURCE: Taeuber, C.M., Population Division, U.S. Bureau of the Census. 1980 Census of Population and Housing, Special Tabulations for NIA.

percent received general welfare assistance. In 1985, more than 90 percent received Social Security benefits, and about 8 percent received general assistance.[68]

Pensions are another important source of income for the older population. Because women are increasingly joining the labor force and because men are increasingly likely to live at least into their seventies, in the future we can expect to see more married couples with two pensions in addition to Social Security benefits.

There are important differentials, however, in pension coverage among various population groups. Pension coverage in 1984 extended to 70 percent of men and 64 percent of women. Only 35 percent of elderly individuals living alone have any pension income.[69] Coverage ranged from only 38 percent of workers with monthly earnings under $500 to 84 percent of those earning $2,000 or more per month. College graduates are more likely to have pensions, and the levels are much higher.[70]

In 1984, one of five pension recipients was a college graduate with an average monthly pension, not including Social Security, of $950, compared with $550 for high school graduates and $330 for those not completing high school. Some 1.8 million persons receiving a pension also worked at a wage or salary job, and their average pension was $730, more than a third higher than that of the 9.7 million retirees who did not work.[71]

Some believe that we are now seeing the "golden age of the golden years,"[72] and that the baby-boom retirees will be less well off than today's retirees. There are many indicators that the personal savings and retirement benefits of the elderly may be less in the future. It is likely however that more of the burden for economic security will fall on the individual.

POVERTY STATUS

The perception of "elderly" and "poor" as practically synonymous has been changing in recent years to a view that "the elderly" are better off than other Americans. Both views are too simplistic. In the early 1960s, about one-third of all elderly had incomes below the poverty level. Partly because of "catch-up" increases and indexing of Social Security to rates of inflation, there have been significant changes nationally. In 1987, 12.2 percent of persons aged 65 years and older were poor. But there are differences in poverty rates among subgroups of "the elderly." For example, poverty increases with age, and the rates are considerably higher for the oldest old. The 1987 poverty rates were higher for elderly blacks (33.9 percent) and Hispanics (27.4 percent) than for whites (10.1 percent).[73]

Data from the 1980 census show that poverty rates among elderly American Indians were similar to those of blacks. The rates for Asians and Pacific Islanders were closer to those of whites (Figure 1-14). Poverty rates are higher in rural areas than urban areas (Figure 1-15). They are lower for white elderly women who do not live with relatives ("unrelated individuals"—most of whom live alone) than for elderly women who are black or Hispanic unrelated individuals. In 1987, the poverty rates for such women were 21.9 percent for whites, 62.8 percent for blacks, and 60.6 percent for Hispanics.[74] Poverty rates in 1979 for persons 85 years and older varied from 11 percent for men living in families to 73 percent of the 30,780 black women who lived alone (Figure 1-16).[75]

Figure 1-14. Percent Poor in 1979 for Persons 65 and Over: 1980

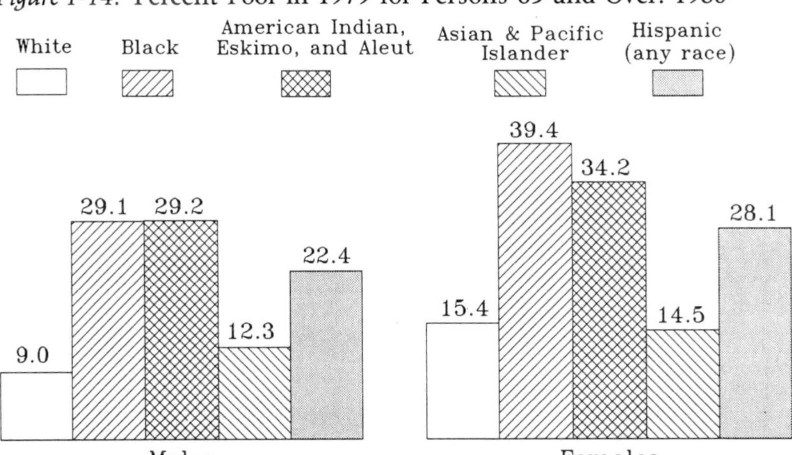

SOURCE: Taeuber, C.M., Population Division, U.S. Bureau of the Census. 1980 Census of Population and Housing, Special Tabulations for NIA.

Figure 1-15. Percent Poor in 1979 for Persons 60 Years and Over by Age, Sex, and Residence: 1980

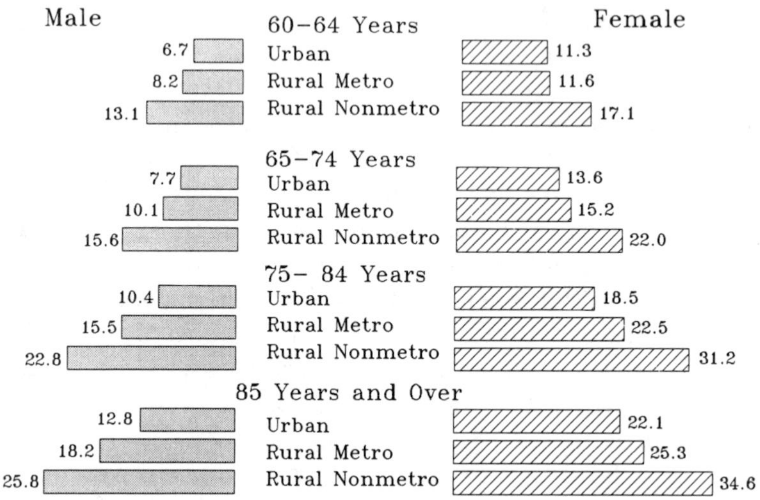

SOURCE: Taeuber, C.M., Population Division, U.S. Bureau of the Census. 1980 Census of Population and Housing, Special Tabulations for NIA.

Figure 1-16. Percent Poor in 1979 for Persons 85 Years and Over: 1980

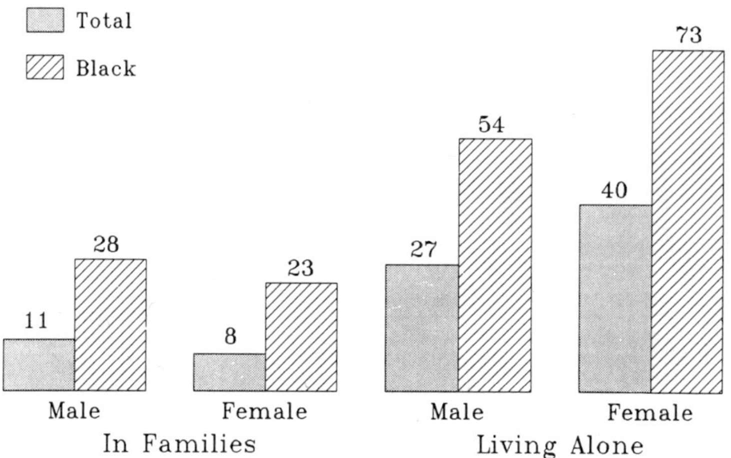

SOURCE: Taeuber, C.M., Population Division, U.S. Bureau of the Census. 1980 Census of Population and Housing, Special Tabulations for NIA.

In short, there are important differences among subgroups of the elderly, and it is fallacious to talk about "the elderly" in sweeping generalizations.

Geographic Distribution and Patterns of Migration

During the 1970s, relatively large communities of elderly became noticeable, not just in the traditional retirement meccas of the Sunbelt, but also in the Ozarks of Arkansas, the woods of northern Wisconsin and Michigan, the mountains of Colorado and Montana, the Puget Sound area of Washington State, the coast of New England, and central Texas. Most states have shown a steady rise in the proportion of elderly persons. Some states "age" because of in-migration of elderly, some because of out-migration of the young, and some because of low fertility (or some combination of these factors).

The states with the largest populations have the largest number of elderly as well as the largest number of the oldest old. In 1987, eight states had more than one million elderly: California, New York, Florida, Pennsylvania, Texas, Illinois, Ohio, and Michigan.[76]

The same states also had the largest populations aged 85 and older. The costs to states of a large elderly population depend greatly on the distribution of the oldest old. As noted by Rosenwaike and others, it is the healthier, higher economic status, and younger old who move to the Sunbelt soon after retirement. It is the frail very old who tend not to move unless it is to a local nursing home or to return to their state of origin.[77]

The Census Bureau projects that by the year 2000, about half of the nation's 35 million elderly will live in the same eight states that had the highest numbers of elderly in 1987, although the order will be somewhat different. California is expected to have the most elderly with 3.8 million persons 65 years and older, an increase of 30 percent from 1987. Florida is expected to have the second highest elderly population with 3.1 million, a 43 percent increase from 1987. New York is expected to be third with almost 2.5 million elderly, with a 7 percent increase from their 1987 estimate of 2.3 million elderly. Alaska has the smallest number of elderly, and only 30,000 are expected to live there in the year 2000.[78]

The states with the greatest *proportion* of elderly are often different from those with the greatest *number* of elderly. Florida, however, with almost 18 percent of its population aged 65 or older, had a large number as well as the highest proportion in 1987. The Farm Belt states also have a higher than average proportion of elderly now (primarily because of out-migration of the young). The states with the highest proportion of persons 85 years and older are Iowa (1.9 percent), South Dakota (1.8 percent), Nebraska (1.8 percent), and Kansas (1.7 percent); all other states had 1.5 percent or lower. Western states such as Colorado, Wyoming, Montana, and Utah usually have relatively low proportions of the elderly and the oldest old.

By the year 2000, according to Census Bureau projections, more than one in five Floridians will be elderly, and in Pennsylvania and Rhode Island (states with low fertility), about one in six persons will be elderly. An additional 19 states will have a higher proportion of elderly than the projected national average of 13.1 percent.

Despite all the discussion about movement, most old people stay put, and this has not changed for several decades at least. About 5 percent of elderly persons moved to a different house in the same county from 1985 to 1986. Only about 2 percent moved far enough to change their county of residence. Of those who move, about half remain within the same metropolitan area. The older population who move between regions have tended to follow a migration flow of the younger population by moving from northeastern states into the South. Census data suggest that the older old who move from Florida back to their states of origin (often New York, Ohio, and others), are older, poorer, and more likely to be widows than those moving to Florida. Thus, states such as Florida benefit by receiving healthier, better-off migrants than the "sending" states, who lose well-off consumers but regain consumers of expensive health and welfare services.[79]

Social and Other Characteristics

The various age, sex, race, and ethnic groups within the older population vary in their social and economic characteristics. In general, however, men are more likely than women to be living in a family setting, and as discussed above, the income level of young-old married couples is much better than that of the oldest old and those who live alone.

MARITAL STATUS AND LIVING ARRANGEMENTS

Living arrangements and marital status shift considerably with advancing age and the patterns differ between men and women. Before age 75, most older Americans are married (with spouse present); the exception is black women. In 1988, among those aged 55 to 74 years old living in households (Figure 1-17), white men were the most likely to be married (83 percent); black women were the least likely to be married (36 percent).[80]

At age 75 and older, among the noninstitutionalized population, men are still most likely to be married, but widowhood is the most common marital status for women. In 1988, two in three white men 75 years and older were married (spouse present and living in the household) while two in three white women that age were widows. As shown in Figures 1-18 and 1-19, black men were more likely than black women to be married as was also the case among Hispanics.[81] Data from the 1980 census show that among persons 75 years and older, Asians and Pacific Islanders (API) and American Indian, Eskimo, and Aleut (AI) men and women had rates of

Figure 1-17. Percentage of Persons Aged 55 to 74 Who Are Married (Spouse Present), by Race and Hispanic Origin: 1988 (noninstitutional population; persons of Hispanic origin may be of any race)

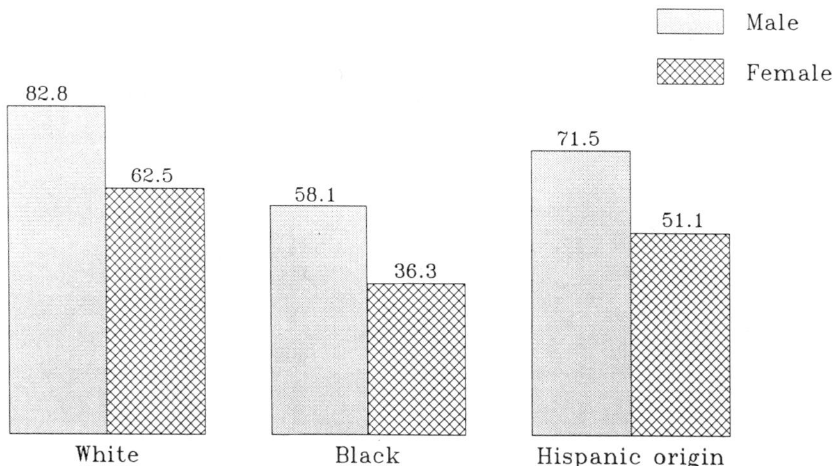

SOURCE: U.S. Bureau of the Census. "Marital Status and Living Arrangements: March 1988," *Current Population Reports*, Series P-20, No. 433. Washington, D.C.: U.S. Government Printing Office, 1989.

Figure 1-18. Percentage of Persons Aged 75 and Over Who Are Married (Spouse Present), by Race and Hispanic Origin: 1988 (persons of Hispanic origin may be of any race)

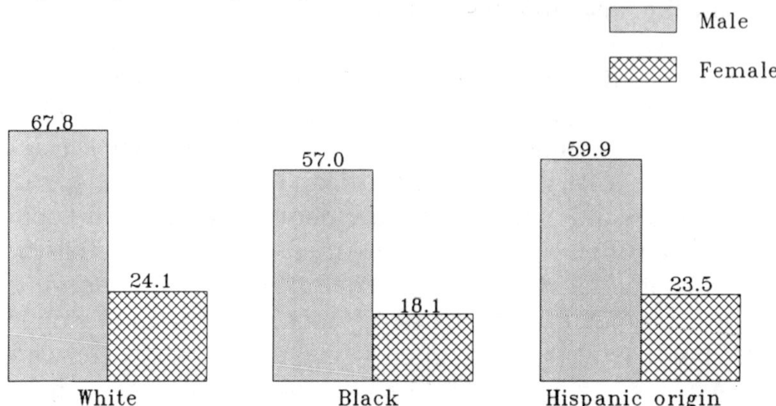

SOURCE: U.S. Bureau of the Census. "Marital Status and Living Arrangements: March 1988," *Current Population Reports*, Series P-20, No. 433. Washington, D.C., U.S. Government Printing Office, 1989.

Figure 1-19. Percentage of Persons Aged 75 and Over Who Are Widowed, by Race and Hispanic Origin: 1988 (persons of Hispanic origin may be of any race)

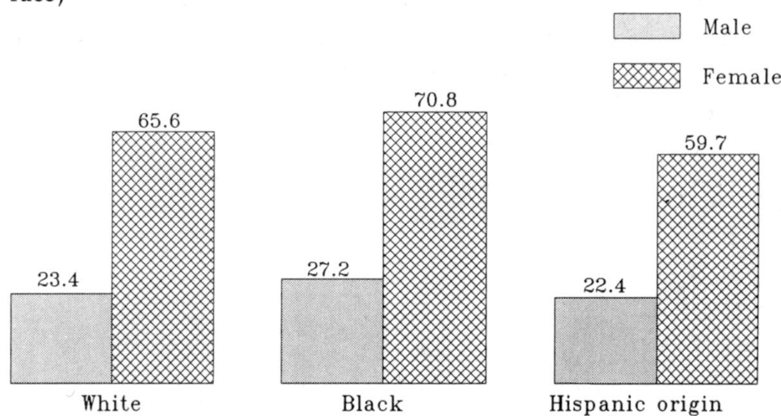

SOURCE: U.S. Bureau of the Census. "Marital Status and Living Arrangements: March 1988," *Current Population Reports*, Series P-20, No. 433. Washington, D.C.: U.S. Government Printing Office, 1989.

widowhood similar to those of other aged persons [men: black (33 percent), AI (32 percent), API (22 percent), Hispanic (27 percent); women: black and API (73 percent), AI (72 percent), Hispanic (68 percent)].[82]

Gains in life expectancy have influenced the chance that a newborn will live long enough to reach marriageable age as well as experience divorce or widowhood. The cohort of men and women born from 1898 to 1912 were somewhat less likely to marry than is the baby-boom generation. According to a model by Schoen et al.,[83] the baby-boom cohorts would be about twice as likely as were the oldest old to experience divorce over their lifetime. Women born at or before the turn of the century were likely to experience widowhood at younger ages than are the women of the baby-boom generation whom the Schoen model projects to experience widowhood, on the average, around age 65. On average, these women live about 15 years as widows. The model projects that less than one in ten will remarry.

There is an increasing likelihood that white men and white, black, and Hispanic women will live alone as they age, especially women. This fact is related to the traditionally shorter life expectancies of men and the tendency of women to marry men older than themselves. Most elderly who live alone are not disabled, are in good or excellent health, and have families nearby and other companionship. About three of five have lived in the same place for ten or more years. Those living alone also have had a greater tendency to use community services than do those living with others.[84]

The average age of those elderly who live alone is about 75 years and most are widows. Three million people aged 55 to 64 lived alone in 1988 (two-thirds were women and just over half were white women) as did 8.7 million persons aged 65 or older (eight in ten were women; seven in ten were white women). Among persons aged 65 to 74 years, about one-third of black and white women lived alone, and they were more likely to live alone than Hispanic men or women (Figure 1-20).[85]

For those 75 years and older in 1988 (Figure 1-21), white women were the most likely to live alone (52 percent); white and Hispanic-origin men were the least likely (21 and 17 percent, respectively, which are not statistically significant differences).[86] Data from the 1980 census show that the proportion of elderly American Indians, Eskimos, and Aleuts living alone (men, 24 percent; women, 42 percent) was close to that of blacks in 1980 (men, 24 percent; women, 40 percent); also, the proportion of elderly Asians and Pacific Islanders living alone (men, 16 percent; women, 37 percent) was more similar to that of Hispanics (men, 17 percent; women, 31 percent).[87]

Figure 1-20. Percentage of Persons Aged 65 to 74 Living Alone, by Race and Hispanic Origin: 1988 (persons of Hispanic origin may be of any race)

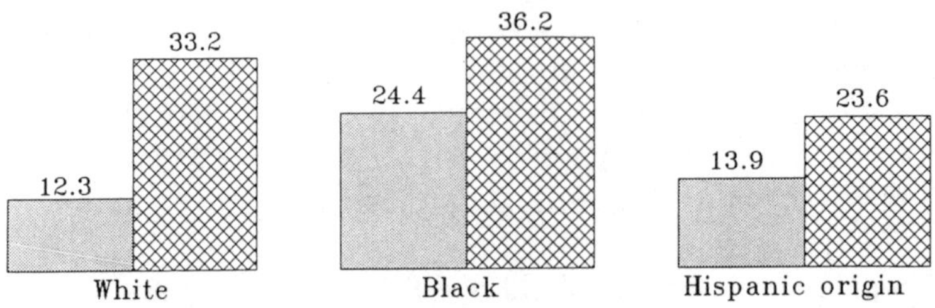

SOURCE: U.S. Bureau of the Census. "Marital Status and Living Arrangements: March 1988," *Current Population Reports,* Series P-20, No. 433. Washington, D.C.: U.S. Government Printing Office, 1989.

Figure 1-21. Percentage of Persons Aged 75 and Over Living Alone, by Race and Hispanic Origin: 1988 (noninstitutional population; persons of Hispanic origin may be of any race)

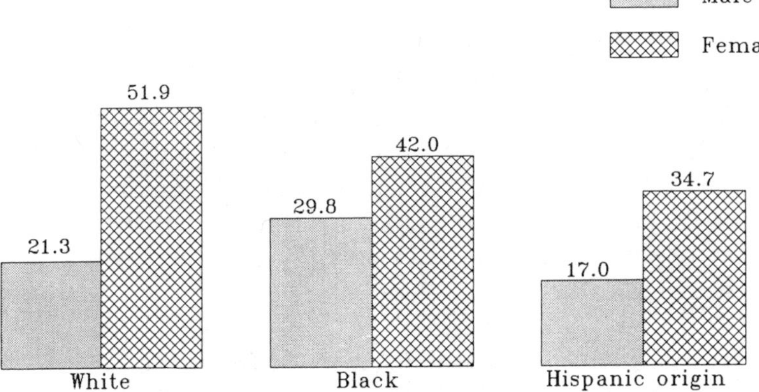

SOURCE: U.S. Bureau of the Census. "Marital Status and Living Arrangements: March 1988," *Current Population Reports,* Series P-20, No. 433. Washington, D.C.: U.S. Government Printing Office, 1989.

For elderly men, there has been virtually no difference over the last two decades in the proportion who live alone (13.0 percent in 1967; 15.6 percent in 1987) or who live in families (83.5 percent in 1967; 81.9 percent in 1987).[88]

It is likely that the trend of an increasing proportion of aged women living alone will continue, and there is also no reason to expect the proportion of men living in families will change much. The Census Bureau projects that by the year 2000 women will maintain over half of the households maintained by persons aged 75 years and older.[89]

Today's young-old women are more likely to be in relatively good health and to be able to afford to live alone than was true in the past. For some, living alone stems from a desire not to be dependent on others; for others, there is no alternative. Women who live alone seem to fare better than men socially and physically, if not economically. For example, women who live alone typically have social contacts and diets similar to those of married couples. Older men, who often do not know how to cook, have less nutritional diets in general.[90, 91] In 1984, of the 17 million persons aged 70 years and older who lived in households, 6 million lived alone, 7 million lived with only their spouse, and 4 million (many with serious health problems) lived with other people. Just over one in five persons seventy years and older who lived alone (1.7 million) in 1984 had no living children. Of those who had living children, nearly half had daily contact and 85 percent had at least weekly contact with their children.[92]

There has been a focus in the literature on the status of those who live alone. Those aged who live with family members other than a spouse, however, often have poorer health than other elderly living in households.

ELDERLY LIVING IN INSTITUTIONS

Most elderly live in households but the likelihood of living in a nursing home increases with age. In 1980, about 1.5 percent of those aged 65 to 74 lived in a nursing home compared with 7 percent of the 75- to 84-year-old group, and 22 percent of those aged 85 years and older. Four of five residents of nursing homes were aged 75 or older and seven of ten were women.[93]

The risk of institutionalization after age 65 may exceed 50 percent,[94] primarily because most admissions are short term (three of four are for less than one year).[95] Families frequently use nursing homes for both recuperative care and care of those near death.

The increasing number of aged and the increased participation of women (the primary caretakers of the aged) in the labor force lead many to believe that the number and proportion of elderly living in institutions will increase. A factor that may mitigate the demographic circumstances is that medical advances and increased understanding of the social-psychological factors that lead to institutionalization could actually decrease the risk of long-term institutionalization. For example, nearly one-fourth of those now in nursing homes are there because of strokes.[96] Medical researchers are determining ways to reduce the severe brain damage that accompanies stroke for many patients, however.[97] Research is trying to identify those with a high risk for institutionalization. Data from the 1984 Supplement on Aging showed that those with strong social networks are the most likely to survive and remain healthy.[98]

Whether the frail elderly receive care in nursing homes or by families or others in the elderly person's home, more and more people will experience the enormous economic, emotional, and physical stress of long-term care for frail elderly persons.

The Elderly of Today and Tomorrow

In an increasingly interdependent and aging world, the United States is remarkable for the diversity of its older population. It is never easy to arrive at a shared vision when there are strong differences, but that is our challenge. The pace and direction of demographic changes will create compelling social, economic, and ethical choices for individuals, families, and governments into the next century.

The coming growth of the elderly population is stunning. As the years proceed, we can expect to see less of our traditional focus on youth. We will need more understanding of our differences and similarities. Already we are searching for answers to essential questions. The directions we choose and the decisions we make will directly affect the quality and vitality of our lives for many decades.

We face questions such as whether more people are at risk for extended years of disability or whether the age of the onset of chronic conditions is going to be postponed. What will happen if large numbers of people have Alzheimer's disease, for example? Is it inevitable? Preventable? How do we balance funding for research to learn how to prevent chronic illness with funding for research to prevent and treat killer diseases? Is there a greater role for educating the public about the long-term effects of life-style? Who will care for the physically and economically dependent aged? How can our care programs take into account cultural differences? Will the older population be able to pay a larger proportion of the costs of their old age?

This chapter describes the older population of today. One lesson that we are learning is that the life one leads as a younger person affects one's prospects in older age. As such, it is wrong to assume that the older population of tomorrow will look the same as the older population of today. A look at the characteristics of younger cohorts can help to predict change. Educational attainment is much higher for the baby-boom generation, for example. Young minorities in the labor force are employed in occupations covered by Social Security and retirement plans more often than is true of their parents.[99] Such characteristics are indicators of the likelihood of eventual differences between today's and tomorrow's elderly in health and economic status.

The key thought we have focused on throughout is that in less than twenty-five years, the United States will have a much larger, more diverse older population. This is a virtual certainty in America and throughout the world. It will happen whether we plan for it or not. It will be a challenge to anticipate the change in needs and desires of a diverse, aging America.

Notes

1. Siegel, S., and C.M. Taeuber. "Demographic dimensions of an aging population." In A. Pifer and L. Bronte (Eds.), *Our Aging Society: Paradox and Promise*, New York: W.W. Norton & Co., 1986, pp. 102-103.

2. Spencer, G., U.S. Bureau of the Census. "Projections of the Population of the United States, by Age, Sex, and Race: 1988 to 2080." *Current Population Reports*, Series P-25, No. 1018. Washington, D.C.: U.S. Government Printing Office, 1989. The Census Bureau produces thirty series of projections based on varying assumptions about fertility, life expectancy, and immigration. Unless stated otherwise, the projections used here are from the "middle series," which assumes 1.8 lifetime births per woman, life expectancy at birth in 2050 of 76.4 years for men and 83.3 years for women, and an ultimate net immigration of 500,000 persons yearly. That is, the middle series does not anticipate any significant changes in any of the components of population change. Projections are *not* forecasts or predictions. If we make no arithmetic mistakes, projections are always "correct" in the sense that they are the accurate results of mathematical calculations based on assumptions. Forecasts are projections that analysts judge to be the most probable end result. It would be contradictory to

make alternative forecasts although it is appropriate to develop numerical ranges for forecast values. Predictions have no formal meaning; they are related more to forecasts than to projections.

3. Torrey, B., K. Kinsella, and C.M. Taeuber, U.S. Bureau of the Census. "An Aging World." *International Population Reports,* Series P-95, No. 78. Washington, D.C.: U.S. Government Printing Office, 1987. All data for this section come from this report.

4. "Developed" countries include all nations in North America and Europe as well as the Soviet Union, Japan, Australia, and New Zealand. The remaining nations of the world are considered "developing" countries.

5. Spencer, G., U.S. Bureau of the Census. "Projections of the Hispanic Population: 1983 to 2080." *Current Population Reports,* Series P-25, No. 995. Washington, D.C.: Government Printing Office, November 1986. Middle series projections.

6. U.S. Bureau of the Census. 1980 Census of Population. *General Social and Economic Characteristics,* PC80-1-C1, U.S. Summary. Washington, D.C.: Government Printing Office, December 1983, Table 120.

7. The number shown is from the middle series and assumes constant immigration consistent with recent levels of legal immigration. If we use an alternative assumption, such as in Series 17, which includes an allowance for undocumented immigration, the number of elderly Hispanics could increase to 10.8 million; of these, 7.5 million would be aged 65 to 79 and 3.3 million would be aged 80 and older.

8. The proportion of elderly who are minorities (that is, Hispanics and races other than white) could be higher than two in ten if many Hispanics identify their race as white (in the 1980 census, about 58 percent of Hispanics, regardless of age, identified their race as white, 3 percent as black, and the remainder as some other race).

9. Rosenwaike, I., and A. Dolinsky. "The changing demographic determinants of the growth of the extreme aged." *The Gerontologist,* 27: 275-280.

10. Under the middle series projections, the population younger than aged 65 would actually decrease by 2.5 percent; the population aged 65 to 84 would grow 72.9 percent; the population aged 85 and older would grow by 32.9 percent. See Spencer, *Current Population Reports,* Series P-25, No. 1018.

11. U.S. Bureau of the Census. "Fertility of American Women: June 1987." *Current Population Reports,* Series P-20, No. 427. Washington, D.C.: U.S. Government Printing Office, 1988.

12. Siegel and Taeuber. *Our Aging Society,* p. 84.

13. Two elderly generation ratio from 2030 to 2050: whites, 45 to 95; blacks, 30 to 67; other races, 43 to 68; Hispanics, 38 to 69.

14. Menken, J. "Age and Fertility: How Late Can You Wait?" Presidential address delivered at the annual meeting of the Population Association of America, Boston, March 28, 1985.

15. Brody, E. M. "Parent care as a normative family stress." *The Gerontologist*, 25: 19–29.

16. Researchers have not determined the relative costs of young and old. See Adamcheck, D.J. and E.A. Friedman. "Societal aging and generational dependency relationships." *Research on Aging*, 5, 3 (September 1983): 319–338.

17. Havlik, R.J., B.M. Liu, M.G. Kovar, et al., National Center for Health Statistics. "Health Statistics on Older Persons, United States: 1986." *Vital and Health Statistics*, Series 3, No. 25, DHHS Pub. No. (PHS) 87-1409, Public Health Service. Washington, D.C., U.S. Government Printing Office, June 1987, p. 3.

18. Fingerhut, I.A., National Center for Health Statistics. "Changes in Mortality Among the Elderly, United States, 1940-1978, Supplement to 1980." *Vital and Health Statistics*, Series 3, No. 22a, DHHS Pub. No. (PHS) 82-1406a, Public Health Service. Washington, D.C.: U.S. Government Printing Office, April 1984.

19. National Center for Health Statistics: *U.S. Decennial Life Tables for 1979-1981*, 1, 1. DHHS Pub. No. (PHS) 85-1150-1, Public Health Service. Washington, D.C.: U.S. Government Printing Office, August 1985.

20. Havlik et al. *Vital and Health Statistics.*

21. Spencer. *Current Population Reports*, P-25, No. 1018, Table B-5, p. 153.

22. National Center for Health Statistics. *U.S. Decennial Life Tables for 1979-81.* Unpublished life table values for Hispanics from G. Spencer, Population Division, Bureau of the Census. Life table values for American Indians and Alaskan Natives from A. Handler, Indian Health Service, "American Indian and Alaskan Native Life Expectancy, 1979-1981," for 28 reservation states (which include 67 percent of American Indians).

23. Havlik et al., *Vital and Health Statistics* Table 1, p. 7.

24. Spencer. *Current Population Reports*, P-25, No. 1018, Table N, p. 13.

25. Havlik et al., *Vital and Health Statistics*, Table 3, p. 8.

26. Havlik et al., *Vital and Health Statistics*, p. 6.

27. Metropolitan Life Insurance. "New Longevity Record in the United States." *Statistical Bulletin*, 69, 3 (July-September 1988): 15.

28. Metropolitan Life Insurance. *Statistical Bulletin*, p. 20.

29. Havlik et al., *Vital and Health Statistics*, p. 20.

30. Ibid.

31. National Center for Health Statistics, average annual rates from the National Health Interview Survey, 1982-84.

32. Callahan, D., *Setting Limits: Medical Goals in an Aging Society*, New York: Simon and Schuster, 1987.

33. Herz, D.E., Bureau of Labor Statistics. "Employment characteristics of older women, 1987." *Monthly Labor Review*, September 1988, p. 3.

34. Ibid., Table 1, p. 4.

35. U.S. Department of Labor. *Employment and Training Report of the President*, sent to Congress in 1981, Table A-3.

36. Bureau of Labor Statistics. *Employment and Earnings*, January 1989, Table 3 (1988 annual averages), p. 162.

37. Tuma, N.B., and G.D. Sandefur. "Trends in the labor force activity of the aged of the United States, 1940-1980," unpublished paper, May 1987.

38. Bureau of Labor Statistics, *Employment and Earnings*, January 1989, Table 3.

39. Herz, *Monthly Labor Review*, p. 4.

40. Bureau of Labor Statistics, *Employment and Earnings*, January 1989.

41. Bureau of Labor Statistics, unpublished tabulations from the 1986 Current Population Survey.

42. Ibid.

43. Taeuber, C.M. and V. Valdisera, Bureau of the Census. "Women in the American Economy." *Current Population Reports*, Series P-23, No. 146. Washington, D.C.: U.S. Government Printing Office, 1986, pp. 18-23.

44. Herz, *Monthly Labor Review*, pp. 5-6.

45. Rones, P.L. and D.E. Herz, Bureau of Labor Statistics. *Labor Market Problems of Older Workers*, Report of the Secretary of Labor. Washington, D.C.: U.S. Government Printing Office, January 1989, p. 38.

46. Ibid.

47. Herz, *Monthly Labor Review*, p. 10 and Table 6, p. 11.

48. Herz, *Monthly Labor Review*, Table 6, p. 11; unpublished data for Hispanics from 1987 Current Population Survey available from D. Herz, Bureau of Labor Statistics.

49. Ibid., pp. 10-11.

50. Taeuber and Valdisera, *Current Population Reports*, Figure 23, p. 22.

51. Bell, D. and W. Marclay. "Trends in retirement eligibility and pension benefits, 1974-1983." *Monthly Labor Review*, April 1987, pp. 18-25.

52. Rones and Herz, *Labor Market Problems*, p. 53.

53. Harris, L. et al. *Aging in the Eighties: America in Transition*, Washington, D.C.: National Council on Aging, 1981.

54. Bureau of Labor Statistics. *Employment and Earnings*, January 1989, Table 33, p. 200.

55. Stein, R.L. and H. Travis. "Labor Force and Employment in 1960." Special Labor Force Report No. 14, *Monthly Labor Review*, April 1961 (Table D-7, p. A-35).

56. Taeuber, C.M., Bureau of the Census. "America in Transition: An Aging Society." *Current Population Reports*, Series P-23, No. 128. Washington, D.C.: U.S. Government Printing Office, 1983, p. 23.

57. Rones and Herz, *Labor Market Problems*, p. 7.

58. Ibid., Table 2, p. 11.

59. Ibid., pp. 6-12, 16-19, 28-33.

60. Ibid., pp. 6-9.

61. Ibid., p. 4.

62. Ibid.

63. Torrey, B. and C.M. Taeuber. "The importance of asset income among the elderly." *Review of Income and Wealth*, Series 32, No. 4 (December 1986): 443-449.

64. Welniak, E., U.S. Bureau of the Census. "Money Income of Households, Families, and Persons in the United States: 1987." *Current Population Reports*, Series P-60, No. 162. Washington, D.C.: U.S. Government Printing Office, 1989, Tables 33 and 34; also P-60, No. 30. The median income of the total population 15 years and over also increased (in constant 1987 dollars, from $14,880 in 1957 for males to $17,750 in 1987; for females, from $4,840 to $8,100). The medians in current 1957 dollars were: males 65+, $1,421; females 65+, $741; males 15+, $3,684; females 15+, $1,199. The 1957–1987 CPI-U factor is 4.03796.

65. Ibid., Figure 16.

66. Glasgow, N., Department of Agriculture, Economic Research Service. "The Nonmetro Elderly: Economic and Demographic Status." *Rural Development Research Report*, No. 70. Washington, D.C.: Government Printing Office, 1988, p. iii.

67. Welniak, *Current Population Reports*.

68. Reno, V. and S. Grad. "Economic security, 1935–1985." *Social Security Bulletin*, December 1985, Tables 12 and 13. Washington, D.C.: U.S. Government Printing Office.

69. Commonwealth Fund Commission on Elderly People Living Alone. "Old, Alone, and Poor." *Overview and Recommendations*, April 16, 1987, p. 1.

70. Nelson, C.T. U.S. Bureau of the Census. "Pensions: Worker Coverage and Retirement Income in 1984." *Current Population Reports*, Series P-70, No. 12. Washington, D.C.: U.S. Government Printing Office, 1987.

71. Ibid.

72. Weinstein, M.H. "The changing picture in retiree economics." Metropolitan Life Insurance, *Statistical Bulletin*, 69, 3 (July-September 1988): p. 7.

73. Littman, M.S. U.S. Bureau of the Census. "Poverty Status in the United States: 1987." *Current Population Reports*, Series P-60, No. 163. Washington, D.C.: U.S. Government Printing Office, 1989, Table 2.

74. Ibid., Table 7, p. 30. The difference is not statistically significant between black and Hispanic women 65 years and older who are unrelated individuals.

75. U.S. Bureau of the Census, special tabulations from the 1980 Census of Population (tabulations funded by the National Institute on Aging), available from C.M. Taeuber, Population Division, Bureau of the Census.

76. Byerly, E., U.S. Bureau of the Census. "State Population and Household Estimates, With Age, Sex, and Components of Change: 1981-1987." *Current Population Reports*, Series P-25, No. 1024. Washington, D.C.: U.S. Government Printing Office, 1988, Table 6.

77. Rosenwaike, I. *The Extreme Aged in America*. Westport, Conn.: Greenwood Press, 1985, p. 66.

78. Wetrogan, S.I. "Projections of the Population of States by Age, Sex, and Race: 1988 to 2010." *Current Population Reports*, Series P-25, No. 1017. Washington, D.C.: U.S. Government Printing Office, 1988, Table 5.

79. Ibid., p. 74.

80. Saluter, A.F. U.S. Bureau of the Census. "Marital Status and Living Arrangements: March 1988." *Current Population Reports*, Series P-20, No. 433. Washington, D.C.: U.S. Government Printing Office, 1989, Table 6.

81. Ibid. Differences between the following groups are not statistically significant: in Figure 1-18, white and Hispanic males, black and Hispanic males, white and Hispanic females, black and Hispanic females; in Figure 1-19, white and Hispanic females, white and black males, white and Hispanic males, and black and Hispanic males.

82. Taeuber, C.M. and D. Smith, Bureau of the Census. "Minority elderly: An overview of characteristics and 1990 census plans," unpublished paper, 1987.

83. Schoen, R., W. Urton, K. Woodrow, and J. Baj. "Marriage and divorce in 20th century American cohorts." *Demography*, February 1985, pp. 101-114.

84. Havlik, et al., *Vital and Health Statistics*, 26-27. Data from National Health Interview Survey 1984 Supplement on Aging.

85. Saluter. *Current Population Reports*. For those aged 65 to 74, the differences between white and Hispanic men and between black men and Hispanic women are not statistically significant.

86. Ibid. Differences between the following groups were not statistically significant: white and Hispanic men; Hispanic and black women; black men and Hispanic women.

87. Taeuber and Smith. "Minority elderly."

88. U.S. Bureau of the Census, "Marital Status and Family Status: March 1967." *Current Population Reports,* Series P-20, No. 170, Tables 4 and 8; "Marital Status and Living Arrangements: March 1987," Series P-20, No. 423, Tables 2 and 6. Washington, D.C.: U.S. Government Printing Office.

89. U.S. Bureau of the Census, unpublished work tables prepared by R. Grymes in conjunction with, "Projections of the Number of Households and Families: 1986 to 2000." *Current Population Reports,* Series P-25, No. 986. Washington, D.C.: U.S. Government Printing Office, 1986. Series B (Middle Series).

90. Riley, M.W. "Aging and Society: Notes on the Development of New Understandings," lecture at the University of Michigan, December 12, 1983, p. 13.

91. Havlik et al. *Vital and Health Statistics,* pp. 26–27.

92. Kovar, M.G. "Aging in the Eighties, People Living Alone—Two Years Later." National Center for Health Statistics, *Advance Data,* No. 149, April 4, 1988, Table 2. Data from the 1984 Longitudinal Survey on Aging.

93. Taeuber, *Current Population Reports,* No. 128, p. 23.

94. McConnell, C.E. "A note on the lifetime risk of nursing home residency." *The Gerontologist,* 24: 193-198.

95. Liu, K. and K. Manton. "The characteristics and utilization pattern of admission cohorts of nursing home patients." *The Gerontologist,* 23: 92-98.

96. National Center for Health Statistics, 1977 National Nursing Home Survey, *Vital and Health Statistic Reports,* Series 13, No. 43, July 1979.

97. Wood, J.H., K.S. Polyzoidis, D.B. Kee, Jr., A.R. Prats, G.L. Gibby, and G.T. Tindall. "Augmentation of cerebral blood flow induced by hemodilution in stroke patients after superficial temporal-middle cerebral arterial bypass operation." *Neurosurgery,* October 1984, pp. 535-539.

98. Kovar, M.G. National Center for Health Statistics. "Aging in the Eighties, People Living Alone—Two Years Later." *Advance Data from Vital and Health Statistics,* No. 149, DHHS Pub. No. (PHS) 88-1250. Washington D.C.: U.S. Government Printing Office, April 4, 1988, p. 1.

99. Taeuber and Valdisera, *Current Population Reports,* p. 22.

CHAPTER TWO

Delivering Services to Elders: Responsiveness to Populations in Need

SANFORD L. KRAVITZ, MARTHA B. PELAEZ, AND MAX B. ROTHMAN

Mounting evidence indicates that older Americans as a group live longer, healthier, and financially more secure lives than at any period in history. Federal, state, and local initiatives on behalf of the elderly, particularly since the 1960s, have dramatically changed conditions that were widespread prior to the passage of the Social Security Act. However, research indicates that many older persons live under conditions that create the opposite of a healthy, economically secure old age.[1] During the latter half of this century, the nation witnessed the feminization of poverty, particularly among older persons. By the 1980s, the condition of older ethnic minorities had made ethnicity as well as gender yet another indicator of frailty, poverty, and need for services.

Many older persons, particularly those with fixed retirement incomes, are increasingly the victims of the shortage of low- and moderate-income housing and the rising costs of health care. The prospect of the catastrophe of a long-term illness and institutionalization of a parent is a haunting specter for many families with aging relatives. Other critical factors, such as geographic location and the absence of caregivers, as well as race and ethnicity, affect the prospect of well-being in the later years.[2]

Ethnicity and Social Need

In any review of the demography of the elderly population, ethnicity is emerging, along with gender, as a key variable in understanding the needs of an aging population. The ethnic minority factor refers to the status and experiences of special populations, such as Hispanics, Native Americans, Asian Americans, African Americans, and other ethnic groups. The numbers of minority older persons have been growing at a much more rapid rate than white elderly. Taeuber in Chapter 1 reports that the elderly black population has grown by one-third in comparison with a 25 percent growth in the number of elderly whites.[3] The number of nonwhite elderly persons, estimated at more than 2 million in 1980, will grow to 4 million by the year 2000. The Hispanic elderly population has more than tripled in the last two decades. The Federal Council on Aging estimates that there will be almost 4 million nonwhite elderly by the year 2000.[4]

Many authors have reported on the common tendency to discuss all minorities as a cohesive group. Concern for equity and civil rights has probably contributed to the use of shorthand or global terminology.[5] Significant differences do exist among ethnic groups and between those who may be counted under a single Census Bureau classification. There are, for example, Hispanics who are recent arrivals from Central America as compared to long-time, more acculturated Hispanic groups. Chicanos, Cubans, and Puerto Ricans are all defined under the same census category, but each group has substantially different cultural experiences. Hispanics include whites and nonwhites. Many white Hispanics prefer to be classified as white rather than Hispanic. Many Jews who come from Latin America prefer to be classified as Jews. Blacks who have lived all their lives in rural areas may experience aging differently from those who live in the inner city ghetto. Some U.S. communities have growing populations of elderly persons from the Caribbean Islands. Asians are classified by the Bureau of the Census as those native Americans or immigrants whose family origins are Asian or Pacific island ethnicities, including Japanese, Chinese, Filipino, Korean, Vietnamese, Hawaiians, Samoans, Asian Indians, and Guamanians. Even among Native Americans, there are wide variations in culture, habitat, and access to resources. These groups reflect populations in which diversity is the norm rather than the exception.

The issue of the diversity in the populations served by human service agencies is not new. As early as 1917, Richmond cautioned caseworkers dealing with immigrants to be careful not to think of them as "members of a colony or of a nationality having . . . fixed characteristics. To ignore national and racial characteristics would be an error . . ."[6]

In using the term *ethnic group* we follow Gordon, who stated that an ethnic group consists of those people who share a unique social and cultural heritage and a historical past. Factors that contribute to ethnicity include an associated sense of peoplehood and identification with the group, as well as factors such as national origin, religion, a common language, and race.[7]

For human service workers in an increasingly ethnically diverse environment, what will be required has been defined as ethnic-sensitive practice.[8, 9] Ethnic-sensitive practice is based on the view that practice must be aligned with the values and dispositions related to ethnic group membership and position in the social stratification system. Green states that efforts aimed at problem resolution must be attuned to ethnically distinctive values and community practices. Norton suggests that ethnic-sensitive practice involves the concept of the "dual perspective." By this is meant the necessity for the worker or helper to perceive, understand, and compare simultaneously the values, attitudes, and behavior of the larger society with those of the client's or patient's immediate family, ethnic environment, and community system.[10]

This is not to suggest that a distinct theory or mode of practice must be developed for each cultural group, but rather that minority group status must be an important consideration in applying a practice theory to a problem.

To examine the needs of a diverse population of older persons and the capacity of service systems to respond to their needs, five scenarios are presented. The scenarios were constructed from interviews with service providers and gerontology specialists who have intimate knowledge of the types of older persons described. The scenarios are totally fictional; however, they mirror real cases. (All case histories are indeed partial elements of situations confronting real people. No case is an actual person or family.)

Each case is an effort, admittedly partial, to look at an older person or family within the context of several critical variables, including ethnicity, race, geographic location, financial resources, availability of caregivers, and the types of problems each presents to the service network. We have chosen a Chinese woman living in the Chinatown section of San Francisco, a black woman in rural Mississippi, a Cuban woman in Miami, a European-born Jewish couple in Philadelphia, and a white man in his fifties living in a midsized city in Ohio. Each has different problems, each has a special set of needs, and yet each demonstrates classic problems that confront many people as they age. They reflect the theme of common needs amidst diversity. Each case illustrates both practice and policy issues confronting service providers.

A Woman in Chinatown, San Francisco

Asians are among the most rapidly growing population groups in the United States. By the year 2000, Asians will represent more than 10 million persons. Two-thirds of this Asian population are Chinese, Filipino, and Japanese.[11] Historically, many of these groups dealt with their social problems through locally based groups with strong ties to the relevant traditional culture, that is, family, kinship, merchant groups, and benevolent societies. As these communities age, it is increasingly clear that the problems that Asian elderly confront approximate the problems of other ethnic groups and require services far beyond the resources of such local ethnically oriented self-help groups. These groups are themselves in a state of transition. As the younger generations move away from traditional roles, values, and expectations and respond to the pressures and demands of the dominant culture, the support base for these traditional groups diminishes.[12]

Ms. Hu Hsueh-Chen

Hu Hsueh-Chen is a 75-year-old widow who immigrated to the United States in 1970 with her husband. She lives in San Francisco's Chinatown. Her home is a tiny room lacking kitchen and toilet facilities. These primitive amenities are shared with six other tenants who live on the same floor. The building, constructed more than 80 years ago, was originally a dormitory for male Chinese workers brought to the United States at the turn of the century. Her rent is $170 per month. The other *tenants in the building are all women, of her age or older. Although they share a common Oriental heritage, they are from different parts of China; some from rural areas and some urban. They do not share the same experiences, living habits, or even dialects. What they do share is their economic circumstances, their substandard housing, their marginality in a larger society that is quite foreign to their previous life experiences.*

Ms. Hsueh-Chen and several of her neighbors are clients of the major social service agency serving Chinatown's elderly, Self-Help for the Elderly. Ms. Hsueh-Chen came to the agency seeking better housing and help with a Social Security problem. She had also heard about the food stamp program, but did not know how to negotiate that system. She and her husband had applied for public housing six years earlier, before he died, and she remains on a long waiting list. No new public housing has been built in San Francisco for several years. The showcase public housing projects for Asians built in the early sixties are now thirty years old; and in fact, an estimated 30 percent of the elderly nationwide live in substandard, deteriorated, or dilapidated housing.

The intake worker at Self-Help is confronted with a classic problem in the service delivery system. Ms. Hsueh-Chen is required to interact with multiple levels of government bureaucracy: the federal Social Security System; a state agency that administers the food stamp program; and the San Francisco Housing Authority, a local agency. How do these entities interact with one another? Ms. Hsueh-Chen could become another hapless victim of the fragmentation of the delivery system.

Ms. Hsueh-Chen's assigned worker will begin work on the Social Security problem by contacting the local office. She will assist in completing a food stamp application. She may be able to resolve these two issues after a time-consuming and vigorous advocacy effort. The housing problem will be much more difficult. The caseworker recognizes that meeting immediate needs is only the beginning. With rheumatoid arthritis and signs of osteoporosis, Ms. Hsueh-Chen is a prime candidate for isolation in her third-floor room. The worker can enroll Ms. Hsueh-Chen in the senior center activity and nutrition program and arrange for Ms. Hsueh-Chen to come to the center three times a week. Ms. Hsueh-Chen will be followed by a case manager, who is Chinese and is sensitive to the cultural nuances of her client. Because of Ms. Hsueh-Chen's medical problems, she will be scheduled for examination at a local health center that has many Asian clients, but few bilingual employees. Many of the staff lack the cultural sensitivity necessary to be able to work with her so that she fully understands the medical terminology, the medications, and the procedures for self-care. Without proper communication by the health professionals as to the nature of her illness, Ms. Hsueh-Chen may not follow the regimen prescribed and her treatment could be compromised.

Too often, health and human services professionals are not sufficiently equipped to deal with the changing demography of an aging society. Relatively few institutions that train health care and human services providers, particularly physicians and nurses, offer specialized training in gerontology. In addition, there is now a compelling need to provide appropriate content in gerontology training programs that will develop understanding of and sensitivity to ethnic and racial differences.

Ms. Hsueh-Chen is poor and speaks limited English. She needs culturally sensitive health care providers and supportive services to help her learn and negotiate the systems in her community and advocacy to help her interact with the separate delivery systems. Supportive services are currently being provided in the form of comprehensive case management, but her case manager is relatively powerless to change her housing situation.

ELDERLY HOUSING: THE NEED FOR OPTIONS

The National Council on Aging has noted in its public policy agenda the serious problems associated with the loss of federal support for housing programs. The dramatic cuts in federal support for housing, along with substantial cuts in service programs, have often forced older persons who are particularly vulnerable because of poverty and ill health to live in housing poorly suited to their needs and without the services that would allow them to continue living in the community.[13]

Housing experts and advocacy groups have stated that there will be a compelling need to improve federal, state, and local cooperation and develop new public and private partnerships. The nation must produce a wide array of housing alternatives such as tax-exempt financing of congregate housing, tax credits to builders, support for home equity conversion, special development efforts in rural areas addressed to housing and housing related services, and support for and expansion of energy conservation and energy support programs.[14]

There are now many well-known housing options for older persons. These include retirement villages, mobile homes, retirement apartments, independent living with support, shared housing, and boarding homes. New modalities are emerging. Advocates argue that housing for the elderly must be integrated with overall community development. They argue that housing for the elderly should be considered more than just building units and should be placed in supportive, safe, and economically viable neighborhoods.[15]

A Black Woman in Rural Mississippi

Older people in rural areas tend to stay where they have spent most of their adult lives. There are more than 500 rural counties in which persons aged 65 and older make up at least 15 percent of the total population. In over half these counties, especially in the nation's heartland, the younger generation has left while the elderly have stayed in place. During the past decade, the largest percentage growth of the elderly population has occurred in rural areas.[16]

The last White House Mini-Conference on Rural Aging pointed out that despite the increasing numbers of the elderly, there are critical unmet service needs in rural areas. Rural towns and villages face issues of transportation, employment opportunity, housing, nutrition, energy, income, mental health and physical health services, social and emotional support systems, and social service delivery. Kaiser et al. cite several studies indicating that the rural elderly experience far greater problems than the urban elderly, regarding the availability, accessibility, and quality of every type of service. They report that the rural elderly experience deficits in every category of services.[17, 18] All of these problems appear to be significantly exacerbated for rural black elderly.[19]

Rural elderly are significantly less well housed than their urban counterparts. They account for 30 percent of all elderly households but suffer twice the incidence of substandard and lower incomes compared with urban elderly households. Their homes, usually much older, are valued at 50 percent of urban houses.

Professional service providers in rural areas report other issues that are less subject to statistical analysis but reflect important cultural factors. The executive director of the Delta Health Center in Mound Bayou, Mississippi, Dr. L.C. Dorsey, describes the rural black elderly of her county as proud, independent, and highly individualistic. She notes that these traits carry over into their health-care-seeking behavior. Rural families may not seek health care if there is no money to pay for it. Dorsey reports that rural black older persons often fail to seek health care because their value system is centered around payment of obligations, and they are very careful about undertaking debts.[20]

Health is defined as freedom from incapacitating disease and the ability to function independently and effectively in relation to age. A worthy goal for the coming decade is the maximizing of the individual health of the nation's older citizens.

Health care also includes the broad issues of access, quality, and appropriateness. As this story about Sally Watson demonstrates, all too often the older person has little or no control over these factors.

Ms. Sally Watson

Ms. Sally Watson is a 78-year-old black woman who lives in Bolivar County, Mississippi. Her home is twenty miles from the county seat. She has five children. Her 60-year-old daughter, her 57-year-old son, and several grandchildren live in Jackson, where her son and daughter are employed by the State Highway Department. Three other children moved to Chicago many years ago. Ms. Watson was the child of sharecroppers and only completed grade school. For much of her adult life, she worked as a domestic for several of the wealthy cotton farmers in the area. Her husband, a farm laborer, was killed in a highway accident twenty years ago. Neither was covered for Social Security benefits. Her three-room frame house is old, but neatly kept and modestly furnished. The crossroads where she lives is a small settlement of some ten houses with a service station and a general store. Most of the other residents in the area are older than 60 and have similar life-styles. She has no telephone and walks to the service station to use the phone when she needs to contact her children.

Her entire life Ms. Watson has endured hard times, hard work, and hard living conditions, but she is a strong-willed person and has been able to survive a great deal of trial and tribulation.

As a younger adult, Ms. Watson received episodic health care. Whatever meager surplus resources existed went to the care of the children. Her life, more recently, has been characterized by denial of physical pain and quiet suffering. Admitting to illness or even thinking about going to a nursing home gives her the sense that she has lost control, that she has given in. Going to a doctor or a clinic is complicated by the difficulties of access, costs, and her long-held belief that home remedies may be better.

Breslow and Somers have described health goals of those persons aged 60 to 74 and 75 and older as follows:[21]

60 to 74 years:

1. *To prolong the period of optimum physical/mental/social activity.*
2. *To minimize handicapping and discomfort from onset of chronic conditions.*
3. *To prepare in advance for retirement.*

75 years and older:

1. *To prolong the period of effective activity and ability to live independently and to avoid institutionalization as long as possible.*
2. *To minimize inactivity and discomfort from chronic conditions.*
3. *When illness is terminal, to assure as little physical and mental distress as possible and to provide emotional support to patient and family.*

These principles are generally acknowledged and should be understood by responsible relatives or caregivers. In this case, Ms. Watson's son and daughter have had a continuing concern about their mother. The daughter arranged to drive her into Mound Bayou for a health checkup at the federally supported Delta Health Center. The examination confirms that she has hypertension with some heart disease, early diabetes, and arthritis. She has lost all her teeth and cannot afford dental care. Many of her ailments are manageable with diet, exercise, periodic checkups, and a careful regimen of medication. Regular oversight by a trained health professional is required. Ms. Watson has no automobile. There is no public transportation to her crossroads home. The Delta Health Center's visiting home health aide, who must cover half of this county, can come for only one hour, one day each week, assuming she has no other emergencies. There are no other locally available senior activities, programs, or services. Ms. Watson has the tiny community church, her few neighbors, and the color television that her children sent her for Christmas for entertainment. With only a Supplemental Security Income (SSI) payment and food stamps, she is among the group of older people living in poverty. The Delta Health Center's federal budget for outreach services to the rural elderly has been systematically cut each year. Many of the resources potentially available to the urban elderly are denied to Ms. Watson and other rural elderly because they are not accessible.

The Health Center's funding cutbacks have dramatically reduced their rural-oriented, disease-prevention, and health-promotion activities. The federal emphasis on funding fee-generating services limits the amount of preventive health care the center can offer to rural patients. There is no state or local program to make up the difference.[22]

Ms. Watson's daughter, with periodic help from her brother, can provide some support. She can occasionally drive Ms. Watson to the Health Center, but without more regular supervision Ms. Watson is about to become a high-risk patient. It is predictable that Ms. Watson will continue to have difficulty and that she is a candidate for more serious complications in the disease entities that she has at present. These diseases are exacerbated by her isolation, her marginal economic support system, the lack of transportation, the distance from quality medical care, and the absence of an accessible social services system.

Ms. Watson is poor, ethnic, and aging in place. She needs health education and disease-prevention assistance. She needs false teeth to improve her nutritional intake. She requires transportation and regular access to health care. The traditional roles of the extended family have been changed by the migration of children to urban areas. To serve her propertly the service system needs to include aggressive outreach and much greater accessibility.

ISSUES OF ELDER HEALTH CARE

As Somers[23] has noted in her recent analysis of wellness programs, the older the population, the greater the focus must be on secondary and tertiary prevention. These definitions are now well understood by most professionals.

Programs to address the health of older Americans must include three components:

- *Primary prevention* is intended to increase individual understanding of health, disease, normal aging and major behavioral risk factors; to foster healthy life-styles; and to improve individual resistance to major diseases.

- The goal of *secondary prevention* is to encourage early detection of specific diseases and to make professional help available when needed.
- *Tertiary prevention* or rehabilitation helps individuals with existing chronic conditions function as independently as possible, avoid complications, and eliminate or forestall the need for institutional care.

For well over a decade, health experts have identified the following familiar themes as problems in health care delivery:[24]

- Demand has outstripped the ability of the system to absorb the increase.
- Costs have dramatically increased inequality of access to care.
- The delivery system has not responded to the challenge of long-term care.
- Prevention, home care, and ambulatory care are not priorities.
- Health professionals are not well distributed between rural and urban areas in ways that might achieve equity in delivery.
- Health and social service systems operate as two distinctly separate systems.

Concern over the federal deficit has recently forced the administration and Congress to institute measures aimed at slowing the growth of federal health outlays. Chief among these was the adoption in 1981 of a diagnosis-related prospective payment system for Medicare, a system that some have charged has resulted in elderly patients being sent home quicker and sicker. Even Medicare's most recent expansion initiative, the Catastrophic Coverage Act of 1988, was promoted as being budget-neutral, financed by additional premiums and a surtax on the well-off elderly.

Since Ms. Watson is ineligible for Social Security benefits, this Medicare reform will have little effect on her life. Rather, she will continue to rely on Mississippi's Medicaid program. While the state is required to pay the premiums that will enroll Ms. Watson in Part B of the Medicare program, any needed inpatient or long-term care services will be funded directly by the state. One of Ms. Watson's primary needs—dentures, to improve her nutritional status—is an uncovered service in both Medicare Part B and in Mississippi's Medicaid program.

The coming decade will continue to be a time of restricted resources and competing demands. Half of the states in the nation now set income standards for Medicaid eligibility for single, aged individuals at or below 77 percent of the poverty level.[25] Those responsible for health policy and program development will have to select programs with a special concern for both health effectiveness and cost effectiveness.[26]

A Woman in Little Havana, Miami

The Hispanic population of the United States has been increasing dramatically.[27] Hispanics are close behind blacks as the nation's second largest minority group. This growth has important implications for the provision of social services. The Hispanic group born in the 1950s will be appearing on the charts as the young old within the next twenty years.[28]

Cubans account for only about 6 percent of the Hispanic population of the United States. However, their elderly constitute 12 percent to 16 percent of all aged Hispanics, which is the largest proportion of elderly among all Hispanic subgroups.[29]

Elderly Cubans, who are predominantly women, are concentrated in South Florida; most reside in Miami. Many live in the high-density, working-class, heavily Cuban sections of the community. Spanish is almost universally spoken, and they feel more comfortable in these Cuban neighborhoods.[30]

Black and Hispanic elderly have twice the likelihood of living in physically inadequate housing as elderly households in general. Ms. Rosa Diaz is among the fortunate elderly who are in the 3 percent who have benefited from government housing programs.

Ms. Rosa Diaz

Rosa Diaz is 79 years old. She was born in Cuba and came to the United States in 1960 with her husband and children. He was a factory worker until his death and she worked as a cleaning woman for ten years. Her daughter is 53 years old and married; she lives in the suburbs and is preoccupied with her own family. Her son, aged 46, is a cocaine addict currently in a residential drug treatment center.

Ms. Diaz lives alone in a federally subsidized housing project. Her income consists of a small Social Security check, food stamps, and modest contributions from her daughter.

Ms. Diaz has never fully recovered from the grief of her husband's death. Her social contacts grow fewer each day as she hesitates to leave her apartment. Two years ago she was victimized and severely injured in a mugging. Her fear of street crime keeps her from visiting friends and attending a nearby Senior Center. She finds it more and more difficult to go shopping and to keep her apartment clean. She suffers from depression, high blood pressure, and failing eyesight. Several physicians at the local neighborhood clinic tried to help her cope with her pain and complaints by prescribing a variety of medications. Most of the time, Ms. Diaz appears confused, depressed, and disoriented. The daughter, beset with her own problems, does not know where to turn. Ms. Diaz could use the assistance of the local Mental Health Clinic. She insists that she is not crazy and says she simply wants to be left alone. Ms. Diaz's physicians tell her children that at their mother's age there is not much that can be done for her. They suggest that the children should start planning for their mother's placement in a more protective environment such as an adult congregate living facility. Their response may reflect their partial view of the situation. Ms. Diaz has not told her physicians or her children that she periodically consults the local "botanica" or herbalist. She has been taking his medicinal materials along with the prescriptions.

At the minimum, Ms. Diaz, as a widow, would need new skills for socialization and for personal management help. She needs a primary care physician who believes in, understands, and practices health promotion and education. She might benefit from a housing manager and housing staff in the public housing project who are knowledgeable and sensitive to the health needs of the elderly. She needs assistance with shopping and housekeeping.

Existing public housing projects are faced with an increasing number of elderly tenants who are less able to care for themselves, but no single agency is ultimately responsible for providing supportive services to the elderly in public housing.[31]

Public housing projects are rarely able to provide any form of personal care services to their elderly residents. Drastic cuts in federal support have also reduced maintenance to a minimum. In the inner city, public housing is often associated with the sale of drugs. In this setting, it is most often the minority elderly who are at the highest level of risk.[32]

Ms. Diaz will need special help to delay premature institutionalization and unnecessary placement in a nursing home.

PREVENTING INSTITUTIONALIZATION THROUGH COMMUNITY SERVICES

The issue of community services to prevent institutionalization is of special importance to those diverse ethnic groups and minorities who are low-income, concentrated in inner cities, isolated by language and culture, and particularly dependent on government-supported services. As this case illustrates, as individual members of these groups age and become increasingly frail, their economic vulnerability is compounded as well. The recent experience of cities such as Miami and San Francisco, in which the older population is getting relatively older, poorer, and ethnically diverse, points to the future prospects for the nation, especially in major metropolitan areas.

These diverse groups share their dependence on state-operated systems. Of paramount importance are access to and quality of services along a continuum of care that, at a minimum, includes health and social services, housing, and transportation.

A recent statewide study in Florida urged that the state attempt to integrate entry into the system of delivery of community services, such as the Older Americans Act and state-funded community care services, with entry into institutional settings, that is, Medicaid-funded nursing homes.[33]

The states now control planning and funding of mental health and health services and increasingly play a pivotal role in housing and transportation. All of these services, essential components of the long-term care system, are difficult to understand and complicated to negotiate even for experienced professionals.

The ability of state government to effectively plan and fund this system at a statewide level is of critical importance. State programs must ensure sufficient flexibility at the community level to accommodate the diverse needs of the various groups. Issues at the community level, such as intake, screening, and case management, take on added meaning for those who are ethnically diverse, poor, frail, and may speak another language. Cultural differences further exaggerate and complicate the use of these complex service-delivery systems. These issues exist in every state and affect all older people who are in need of long-term care. The special needs of ethnic minorities, however, add even greater challenge for those who work to address them.

The direct-service practitioner as well as the service manager is directly affected by these larger issues of service organization.

A Middle-Class White Couple in Philadelphia

The cases described focus on elderly at the margins of poverty. It is essential to understand that social services are not for the poor alone. Those in need are not characteristically persons of color or of a particularly disadvantaged ethnic group. The need for services must also be seen as a necessary accompaniment to the character of life in our society. That character of life is now often defined by dispersed families, changing neighborhoods, multilevel service systems, street crime, and an often widely held assumption that "public goods" or what have also been called social utilities—that is, services—can be left to the vagaries of the marketplace.

Regardless of a history demonstrating a previous capacity for successful functioning under circumstances regarded as "typical" or "normal," several authorities believe that there must be a service system that reaches elders who are themselves neither poor nor disabled but who may be caring for a person who is now prey to the insults of age. That system, many believe, should be part of a universal system of benefits, or available on a fee-for-service basis.[34, 35]

Nathan and Rachel Morris, described in the following case study, are about to seek help and support from the long-term care subsystem.

Long-term care consists of diagnostic, preventive, therapeutic, rehabilitative, supportive, and maintenance services for individuals who have chronic physical and/or mental impairments. These services may be provided in a variety of settings including homes as well as institutions, with the goal of promoting the optimum level of physical, social, and psychological functioning.[36]

This definition of long-term care takes in the following elements: persons to be served, the settings, the services to be offered, and the goal of such services. The organization, planning, and delivery of long-term care services for low-income persons is essentially a responsibility of state governments. In the absence of federal policy, but in the presence of multiple federal and state funding sources, programs, and regulations, the states have struggled to better integrate their systems at statewide and community levels.

The Congress has also been struggling for some time with the issue of a national policy for long-term care. Policy analysts, as well as advocacy groups, have sought to project a funding base on which more adequate services could be built. More than likely, the states will continue to maintain primary responsibility for planning and service delivery of long-term care through the next decade.[37]

While the debate continues, service providers will be faced with the task of responding to the growing demand for services such as those that the Morris family will require.

Nathan and Rachel Morris

Nathan Morris is Jewish and was born in Poland. He immigrated to the United States at age 16. He is 77 years old, and lives with his wife, Rachel, in the Germantown section of Philadelphia. Their home is a comfortable, pleasant, well-furnished two-bedroom apartment in an area that was middle class but is now slowly deteriorating. They have lived there for twenty-five years. Their immediate housing conditions are quite adequate, but housing for the elderly cannot be examined apart from the broader environmental factors affecting older people. Environment goes beyond the room, the home, the public housing project. Environment must also consider shopping, health and human services facilities, networks of friends and neighbors, proximity to caregivers, fear of crime, and transportation.

Mr. Morris retired twelve years ago from his job as a cutter in a men's suit manufacturing plant. Through the years, he was an active union member. Retirement brought a union-negotiated pension that, with his Social Security and savings, has allowed Mr. Morris and his wife to live at an adequate standard without the imminent fear of poverty hanging over their heads.

Mr. and Mrs. Morris have three children. All are professionals who are married and long ago moved to different parts of the country to pursue their careers and raise their families. They regularly telephone, but rarely come back to Philadelphia. Until recently, Mr. Morris and his wife traveled to visit each of their children about once a year.

During the past two years, Mrs. Morris has gradually exhibited symptoms of confusion, memory loss, and disorientation. She cannot bathe or dress herself without the assistance and supervision of her husband. Her physician has told Mr. Morris that her symptoms could be the onset of Alzheimer's disease, and he will refer her for a more complete examination at the major medical center.

Mr. Morris is not prepared for this emotionally. He does not know where to turn for professional counseling and is worried about whether their medical insurance will cover the costs of care for his wife. Their friends in the neighborhood are moving away. Several have died. He has not shared this situation with his children and does not yet understand it himself. He worries about their response and wonders which of them will agree to help. He senses that he is slowly moving toward a crisis, and his traditional social network of family, friends, and former coworkers may not be capable of providing the support he now needs. He may need a new residence. He may need some relief from the demands of care to meet his own needs. He believes he will soon require outside help to provide personal care to his wife as well as help with the housekeeping as he begins to assume more of these unfamiliar tasks himself.

If Mrs. Morris has Alzheimer's, or a related dementia, he will need counseling and the help of a support group to weather the emotional impact. He now needs help to manage the issues of future medical costs and the prospect of future custodial care for his wife. He may be forced to move with his wife to a strange city to be closer to his children, but he will be far from his long-time friends. Here is Nathan Morris, still healthy, alert, active, and responsible, but with large burdens to carry.

Nathan Morris is middle class with good union-related retirement benefits and some elements of a support system in his union and few remaining friends. He needs informed physicians and an Alzheimer's support group. He will require legal and financial counseling to learn how to prepare for his wife's incapacity. He needs education and training in how to maintain Mrs. Morris at home. He may be able to manage with the help of a personal care worker, a day care center, and sharing experiences with other members of a support group. He needs to be counseled on how best to involve his family as the disease progresses.

Mr. Morris is fortunate in that Pennsylvania has an established case-management system to service the needs of long-term care clients.

State governments are in a unique position to confront the challenge of long-term care. Several excellent studies point a clear direction.[38, 39] *There is adequate documentation regarding the compelling need. Public support is strong for policies that ensure the availability of a broad array of long-term care services that do not impoverish older persons and their families.*

The demographic imperatives indicate the need for health and human services professionals, in close alliance with legislators and appointed public officials, to undertake the difficult task of reassessing and realigning the relationships among the diverse elements in the several systems and then establish the policies and programs that will effectively serve the public and make efficient use of scarce resources.

A Young-Old Man in Ohio

The desire for the "young old" to remain involved and active is supported by numerous studies as well as the experience of new programs. A recent Yankelovich survey, "Aging in America," reveals some sobering data.[40]

Middle-aged Americans, the near old, characterize their lifestyle as hectic, frantic, and stressed. "Real" retirement by today's definition is not an aspiration of middle-aged Americans. This, despite the fact that many are leaving the work force at age 55.

The middle-aged in the Yankelovich study sample share the view that successful aging is characterized by staying active. Many do not believe they will have the economic option to stop working. The ideal for middle-aged Americans is to be able in their later years to pursue a second or third career rather than continue what they are doing.[41]

Education as part of the broader field of social welfare was institutionalized as early as the 1940s with the development of senior centers. Education was a means of maintaining wellness and eliminating isolation.[42] The "Lifelong Learning Act," which was passed with the Education Amendments of 1976, set a high goal of educational opportunity. Citizens were to be empowered to engage in lifelong learning "without regard to restrictions of previous education or training, sex, age, handicapping condition, social or ethnic background, or economic circumstances."[43]

Despite the laudable intent of the legislation, the weight given to providing educational resources for older persons must compete with growing demands for health care, housing, nutrition, social services, crime prevention, and transportation services. The question of how the nation can best utilize healthy, energetic, productive human beings—the older person—will follow us into the next decade.

Mr. Samuel Parsons

Samuel Parsons of Urban City, Ohio, is 55 years old. He is employed as a certified public accountant by a national accounting firm at its office in a midwestern, medium-sized city. He is married and has three children. His wife, a high school social studies teacher, is also 55 years old.

Mr. Parsons has been with this company for thirty years and has accumulated sufficient retirement benefits. He wants to consider a new career. He has enjoyed the people contact of his own career and has thought about some kind of social service or counseling work. He has served as a United Way volunteer, and he has some knowledge of human service agencies in the community. He does not want to enter a formal degree-oriented training program in which the other students would be much younger. He would like to explore different options before making a decision. He and his wife have also considered working as a husband-wife team.

He has called the offices of the public school adult education program, the continuing education department of the community college, and the admissions office of the state university. Several of these programs now offer counseling to female homemakers returning to the labor market, but those to whom he spoke were not able to offer Mr. Parsons the specific kind of assistance he felt he needed to seriously explore a new career.

What Mr. and Mrs. Parsons may need is a vocational counseling service that will help them inventory their skills, explore the possibilities of alternative careers, and identify the right kind of training programs that could prepare them to enter their second careers. They need to find an agency or organization to provide such counseling and guidance. They need to determine the seriousness of their own interests, the implications of changing life-style, and the reality of employment opportunities in the second careers they may choose.

EDUCATION FOR OLDER ADULTS

If the Yankelovich data are on the mark, the kinds of assistance needed by the Parsons family may not be generally available in most communities to satisfy what will clearly be a growing need.

In preparation for the next decade, one might revisit the recommendations of an earlier White House Conference prepared under the leadership of Bernice Neugarten.[44] It was recommended that more emphasis be placed on demonstrating the contribution education for older adults can make toward a more just society, rather than arguing for the political or moral right older persons have for continued education throughout the life span.

Education is not to be equated with other social demands. Rather, it is to be perceived as a tool for meeting individual needs while also complementing the needs of the society.[45]

Proponents of lifelong learning argue that education for older persons should be based on the belief that investing in healthy, energetic, productive human beings for whom society can find no use—retirees—is a responsible and cost-effective way of solving some of the unmet needs of society at large. High-quality training programs empowering older persons to take greater responsibility for their personal and financial needs both satisfy the individual's desire for personal dignity and maximize society's resources. Finally, education for older persons is justified for its role in enabling human beings, whether young or old, to pursue the search for meaning in life and to become all that they are capable of becoming. Both of these goals are important components of mental as well as physical health.

Summary: Diversity and the Common Thread

The venerable Ollie Randall, an early leader in studies of older persons, noted that generalizations about this country's older population can be misleading. She said, "Today's 'elderly' are often inaccurately lumped into one group. . . . We are different entities, individuals and individualistic, each as different as one snowflake from another."[46] While this principle is important to remember when discussing responsiveness to populations in need, it is equally important to examine those aspects of this highly diverse population that reflect common threads.

The scenarios described illustrate the wide range of issues that impact the elderly:

- Almost 9 million persons older than age 65 live alone. Most of them are women.
- The income of elderly women is only 57 percent of that of elderly men.
- The diversity of minorities and ethnic groups, who often have very low incomes, increases the need for formal services.
- About one-fourth of all Americans who are older than 65 have chronic health problems that require help from others.
- Adequate housing and/or home-related services are central to the viability of many older persons.[47–50]

Reviewing these case scenarios makes it clear that the problems facing older persons will be exacerbated in the coming decade. Every year the need to develop more rational and effective organization and delivery of personal care services becomes more important, regardless of issues of ethnicity or geographic location. Persons engaged in direct care of the elderly, social agencies and health agencies, and political leaders at all three levels of government will have to confront the problems facing our present organization of service-delivery systems.

In four of the five scenarios, the issue of health care, including availability, access, and responsiveness to cultural and ethnic needs of patients, is clearly present.

Housing availability, housing choice, and freedom of movement are issues that will confront the elderly client and the professional attempting to meet the client's needs.

Again, in four of the five scenarios the issue of long-term care, if not imminent, looms in the background. Ms. Diaz, for example, will, in this decade, join the almost 300,000 other Floridians who are older than age 85. The issue of long-term care will confront her family, her case manager, the social agencies, and the political leadership of the state. Policies regarding long-term care in her state will very much affect what resources will be available to her.

For the growing number of near old who are choosing a second or third career, the choice may be voluntary, as in the case of Mr. Parsons, or it may be involuntary as people discover they can no longer find or keep the kind of job they have always held. In either case, this phenomenon which has affected only a small minority, can be expected to increase exponentially. Social agencies and educational institutions can expect to find Mr. Parsons and perhaps his "structurally unemployed" cousin at their door.

What is the worker to do? How does the social agency respond? What should the policymaker understand about these issues of common needs amidst diversity?

In this examination of five classic scenarios, it is clear that these older persons share a major thread of common need despite their ethnic and geographic diversity. The appreciation for the growing diversity in the older population must be reflected in the quality of training that service providers receive and must be shared by political leaders, policymakers, and program planners as well as direct service staff. Health and human services need to be offered with what has been termed "exquisite sensitivity" to race, language, ethnic origin, and other aspects of culture. This sensitivity must encompass such cultural factors as an unwillingness to face dependency, reliance on herbal medicines, the reluctance to share problems with one's grown children, and language barriers.

Major tasks face this nation in health, long-term care, housing, and education. In each area there must be major policy advances and plans for increasing investment by both the public and voluntary sectors. With greater responsibility shifted to the states and to local levels, there are many opportunities for program improvement, particularly in state government. The most critical tasks are to examine the organization of the services system, restructure methods of funding, and improve cooperation among layers of government.

Yes, Ollie Randall, there is enormous diversity, but there is also common human need to be served with respect, understanding, and uncommon vigor.

Notes

1. U.S. Senate Special Committee on Aging, in conjunction with the American Association of Retired Persons and The Federal Council on Aging. *Aging America: Trends and Projections.* Washington, D.C.: Special Committee on Aging, 1986.

2. Dobelstein, W. and A.B. Johnson. *Serving Older Adults: Policy, Programs and Professional Activities.* Englewood Cliffs, N.J.: Prentice-Hall, 1985, pp. 10-19.

3. C.M. Taeuber, Bureau of the Census. "America in Transition: An Aging Society." *Current Population Reports,* Series P-23, Special Studies. Washington, D.C.: U.S. Department of Commerce, 1983.

4. U.S. Senate Special Committee on Aging. *Aging America.*

5. McNeely, R.L. and J.L. Colen (Eds.) *Aging in Minority Groups.* Beverly Hills, Calif.: Sage Publications, 1983, p. 18-20.

6. Richmond, M.E. *Social Diagnosis.* Glencoe, Ill.: Free Press, 1917, p. 382.

7. Gordon, M.M. *Assimilation in American Life.* New York: Oxford University Press, 1964.

8. Devore, W. and E.G. Schlesinger. *Ethnic Sensitive Social Work Practice.* St. Louis, Mo.: C.W. Mosby, 1981.

9. Green, J.W. *Cultural Awareness in the Human Services.* Englewood Cliffs, N.J.: Prentice-Hall, 1982.

10. Norton, D.G. *The Dual Perspective: Inclusion of Ethnic Minority Content in the Social Work Curriculum.* New York: Council on Social Work Education, 1978.

11. McNeely and Colen, *Aging in Minority Groups,* pp. 29-30.

12. Lee, S.S. and A.K. Lee. "Development of community-based health services for minority elderly in Boston's Chinatown. *Pride Institute Journal of Long-Term Health Care* 7 (Fall 1988): 3.

13. *Perspectives on Aging* 17 (March/April 1988): 8.

14. Bratt, R.D., C. Hartman, and A. Meyerson (Eds.) *Critical Perspectives on Housing.* Philadelphia: Temple University Press, 1986, pp. 362-376.

15. Sherman, S.R. "Housing." In *Handbook of Gerontological Services,* A. Monk (Ed.) New York: Van Nostrand Reinhold, 1985: 385-388.

16. Kaiser, M.A., H.J. Camp, and J. Gibbons. "Services for the rural elderly: A developmental model. *Journal of Gerontological Social Work* 11 (1987): 28-31.

17. Ibid.

18. Ibid.

19. Ibid.

20. Dorsey, L.C., Executive Director of the Delta Health Center, Mound Bayou Mississippi, 2/17/89 interview by author.

21. Breslow, L. and A.R. Somers. "The lifetime health monitoring program: A practical approach to preventative medicine." *New England Journal of Medicine* 296 (1977): 601-608.

22. Dorsey, L.C. "Issues and problems of rural health care." Paper presented to the National Advisory Committee on Rural Health, Jackson, Mississippi, January 23, 1989.

23. Somers, A.R. "Health, wellness and Florida: Health promotion, disease prevention/65." In M.B. Rothman, M.J. Dluhy, A.M. Gilbert, and S.L. Kravitz. (Eds.) *Meeting the Challenge: Organizational and Policy Imperatives for Long-Term Care in Florida*. North Miami: Southeast Florida Center on Aging, Florida International University, 1987, p. 23.

24. Bracht, N.F. *Social Work in Health Care: A Guide to Professional Practice*. New York: Haworth, 1978, pp. 38-39.

25. *Perspectives on Aging*, p. 16

26. Somers, *Meeting the Challenge*, p. 34.

27. McNeely and Colen, *Aging in Minority Groups*, pp. 50-56.

28. Ibid.

29. Ibid.

30. Ibid.

31. U.S. Senate Special Committee on Aging, *Aging America*, pp. 144-146.

32. Encyclopedia of Social Work, 18th ed. Silver Spring, Md: National Association of Social Workers, 1987, pp. 100-101.

33. Somers, *Meeting the Challenge*, II:1.

34. Dobelstein and Johnson, *Serving Older Adults*, pp. 226-233.

35. For a full discussion of the concept of reorganized local social service delivery systems see *Toward a Caring Society*, the report of the U.S. Study Team on its visit to England, Scotland, and Wales. Note, particularly, the report of the rapporteur, Dr. Robert Morris, Columbia University School of Social Work, 1974, 83-94.

36. Somers, *Meeting the Challenge*, II:1.

37. Meltzer, J.F., F. Farrow, and H. Richman (Eds.) *Policy Options in Long-Term Care.* Chicago: University of Chicago Press, 1981.

38. Somers, *Meeting the Challenge,* II, Bib 3-29.

39. Dobelstein and Johnson, *Serving Older Adults.*

40. John and Mary R. Markle Foundation. *Aging in America.* New York: John and Mary Markle Foundation, 1988.

41. Ibid. 22-25.

42. Lowy, L. and D. O'Connor. *Why Education in the Later Years.* Lexington, Mass.: Lexington Books, 1968.

43. U.S. Code Congressional and Administrative News, 94th Congress, 2nd Session, 1976, 90 Stat. 2086-2089.

44. Lowy and O'Connor, *Why Education in the Later Years.*

45. White House Conference on Aging, Final Report. Washington, D.C.: White House Conference on Aging, 1981, 2: 92-93.

46. Quoted in *Perspectives on Aging* 17 (March/April 1988): 5.

CHAPTER THREE

The Politics and Economics of Aging and Diversity

ROBERT H. BINSTOCK

Diversity among aging Americans has been obscured for many decades by stereotypes concerning old people. Although such stereotypes have changed in recent years, the elderly are still perceived as a relatively homogeneous group. As a consequence, those subgroups within the elderly population who experience the most severe conditions of economic and social disadvantage are hidden by images and statistical averages that currently portray the aging, for instance, as "more prosperous than the general population."[1]

Public spending on benefits to the elderly is sizable, both in absolute and comparative terms. Social Security and Medicare alone accounted for $341.4 billion in estimated expenditures, or 29.4 percent of the budget that President Bush submitted to the Congress for fiscal year 1990; compare this with a proposed military budget of $300.4 billion, or 25.8 percent.[2] But the policies through which these funds are expended are not structured so as to substantially ameliorate conditions of extreme hardship experienced by some subgroups of the aging.

Are the severely disadvantaged elderly likely to be helped effectively by the mass political power of older persons and the organizations that represent them? Has Congress recently shown any inclination to target more substantial resources to the disadvantaged aging? As the next White House Conference on Aging approaches, what are the prospects and possible strategies for achieving greater diversity in policies toward the aging?

Compassionate Ageism and the "Old Age Welfare State"

Public policy issues concerning older Americans have been framed for a long time by an underlying *ageism*[3]—the attribution of the same characteristics, status, and just deserts to a heterogeneous group that has been artificially homogenized, packaged, labeled, and marketed as "the aged." Ageism, in contrast with racism, has provided many benefits for older persons.[4]

From the Townsend Movement of the 1930s until about ten years ago, several categorical stereotypes concerning older persons were axioms of public rhetoric in America. These were compassionate stereotypes. Simply put, they were:

- The aged are poor, frail, and perceived in negative terms; hence, they are in need of collective assistance and positive image-building.
- The aged are relatively impotent as a political force, so their advocates should help to develop "senior power."
- The aged are "the deserving poor" because their disadvantaged plight is forced on them by mandatory retirement, the frailties and disabilities of old age, and the prejudices of a youth-oriented society. Consequently, with this rationale satisfying the work ethic in American political ideology, there is no reason why a wealthy American society should not do more for them.

These compassionate stereotypes of older persons masked the many differences among individuals and subgroups. American society accepted the notion that all older persons are essentially the same, and all in need of governmental assistance.

DEVELOPMENT OF PROGRAMS FOR THE AGING

The American polity took the next logical steps. It adopted and financed major age-categorical benefit programs and tax and price subsidies for which eligibility is not determined by need. Through Social Security, Medicare, the Older Americans Act, and a variety of other measures, older persons became exempt from the screenings that are applied to other Americans in order to determine whether they are worthy of public help.

During the 1960s and 1970s, just about every issue or problem affecting some older persons that could be identified by advocates for the aging became a governmental responsibility: nutritional, supportive, and leisure services; housing; home repair; energy assistance; transportation; help in getting jobs; protection against being fired from jobs; special mental health programs; a separate National Institute on Aging; and on, and on, and on.[5] In short, by the late 1970s, if not earlier, American society had learned the catechism of compassionate ageism very well and had expressed it through a variety of governmental programs and objectives that constituted an "old age welfare state."[6] We had rejected proposals for universal national health insurance, for example, but—through Medicare—we were willing to establish national health insurance for the elderly.[7]

Due in great measure to these policies, through which our national government spends 26 percent of its annual budget,[8] the aggregate situation of older Americans has improved dramatically over the years. Social Security has been remarkable in helping to reduce the proportion of elderly persons in poverty from about 35 percent three decades ago[9] to 12.8 percent today.[10] For over two decades Medicare and Medicaid have provided all older persons with public insurance coverage for a great many health care services to which they might not otherwise have had access. The Age Discrimination in Employment Act, through its 1978 and 1986 Amendments, has eliminated mandatory retirement in most sectors of American society. The Older Americans Act of 1965 has provided needed services to countless older persons. The Employee Income Retirement Security Act of 1974 now helps to protect pension benefits for workers who have earned them through years of employment. One could go on and on with respect to how national, state, and local policies—such as subsidized housing, low-income home energy assistance, legal services, home care, and transportation—have reduced vulnerability among older Americans.

CONTINUING VULNERABILITY AMONG THE AGING

Even in the context of these ameliorative policies, however, many older persons remain highly vulnerable with respect to income, health, functional status, and other dimensions of fundamental well-being. This vulnerability will persist, and probably increase, unless national policies are reformed. The very structure of some programs that provide benefits to the aged helps to ensure that life-course inequalities of status will be perpetuated into and throughout old age.[11–13]

Consider, for example, the poor economic status of some older persons. Despite the roughly $300 billion our national government expends annually in benefits to the aging, some 3.6 million older persons have an annual income that is below the government's official poverty line. An additional 4.4 million persons aged sixty-five and older are in households that have annual incomes between the poverty level and 150 percent of that level—in other words, within a few hundred to a few thousand dollars of poverty.[14] This latter subgroup has been dubbed "the 'tweeners" by Smeeding,[15] because on the one hand they are not poor enough to qualify for Medicaid and other means-tested public programs, but on the other hand are not well enough off to be financially secure. These 'tweeners are highly vulnerable to unexpected high-cost health care bills and sudden inflation in housing costs.

The subgroups of older persons most heavily represented in low-income categories are blacks and females. For instance, among older persons living as "unrelated individuals" the percentage of black women in poverty is 60 percent, compared with 24 percent for white women and 17 percent for white men.[16]

Unless national policies are changed substantially in the years immediately ahead, such clusters of older persons who are extremely vulnerable with respect to economic status will not disappear. The eligibility and benefit structures of the Old Age Insurance (OAI) program of Social Security are based on the labor force record of potential recipients. Persons who do not have a long and stable history of employment, or who worked in jobs in which Social Security taxes were not paid, receive very low OAI benefits or do not qualify for them at all. Still others receive benefits that are not sufficient for an adequate income in retirement.[17] Consequently, although Social Security has saved tens of millions of older Americans from poverty, and will continue to do so in the years ahead, its program structure is such that millions more older persons will remain vulnerable to poverty because of their limited work histories within the Social Security system.

While the federal Supplemental Security Income (SSI) Program provides a minimum guaranteed federal income payment averaging $187 per month to older persons who qualify through means test,[18] most estimates are that only 40 to 60 percent of those who are eligible for it apply. Reasons for this lack of participation are not precisely clear, but researchers have suggested a variety of possible factors. These include ignorance of the program; distaste for the stigmatization of being a welfare recipient; the severity of asset and income tests that are applied to determine eligibility; and the small marginal value of the income to be obtained through SSI payments.[19–22] For most of those who do receive SSI payments the amount is not sufficient to bring their incomes up to the poverty line, even in communities where the state government supplements the federal payment.

These are but a few examples of how older persons can remain vulnerable within the context of national policies designed to provide income in old age. As illustrated in this discussion, particularly vulnerable are older women and black, Hispanic, Asian/Pacific, and Native American minorities who, in addition to problems of income, confront gender and racial barriers throughout many dimensions of their everyday lives.

The Emergence of the Aged as Scapegoat

Increasingly during the past decade such continuing vulnerabilities—to poverty, ill health, isolation, gender discrimination, racial and ethnic barriers, and other difficult circumstances—have been lost in public discourse and imagery. Since 1978 the long-standing compassionate stereotypes of older persons have been undergoing an extraordinary reversal[23] through which older persons have come to be portrayed as one of the more flourishing and powerful groups in American society, and attacked as a burdensome responsibility.

The immediate precipitating factor seems to have been a so-called crisis in the cash flow of the Social Security system, within the larger context of a depressed economy during President Jimmy Carter's administration. But regardless of the specific cause, the reversal of stereotypes has continued unabated since then to the point where we now find—in the media, political speeches, public policy studies, and the writings of scholars—a new set of axioms:

1. The aged are relatively well-off—not poor but in great shape.
2. The aged are a potent political force because there are so many of them and they all vote in their self-interest; this "senior power" explains why more than one-quarter of the annual federal budget is spent on benefits to the aged.
3. Because of demographic changes, the aged are becoming more numerous and politically powerful and will claim even more benefits and substantially larger proportions of the federal budget. They are already costing too much and in the future will pose an unsustainable burden on the American economy.

These new stereotypes, devoid of compassion, can be readily observed in popular culture. Typical of contemporary depictions of older persons is a recent cover story in *Time* entitled "Grays On the Go."[24] It is filled with pictures of senior surfers, senior swingers, and senior softball players. Older persons are portrayed as America's new elite—healthy, wealthy, powerful, and "staging history's biggest retirement party."

A dominant theme in such accounts of older persons is that their selfishness is ruining the nation. *The New Republic* highlighted this motif early in 1988 with a cover displaying "Greedy Geezers." The table of contents "teaser" for the story that followed announced that "The real me generation isn't the yuppies, it's America's growing ranks of prosperous elderly."[25]

In serious forums of public discourse, these new stereotypes of the prosperous, hedonistic, and selfish elderly have laid a foundation upon which the aged have emerged as a scapegoat for an impressive list of American problems. As social psychologist Gordon Allport observed in his classic work the *ABC's of Scapegoating*: "An issue seems nicely simplified if we blame a group or class of people rather than the complex course of social and historical forces."[26]

Demographers[27] and advocates for children[28] have blamed the political power of the elderly for the plight of youngsters who have inadequate nutrition, health care, education, and supportive family environments. Former Secretary of Commerce Peter Peterson[29] has suggested that a prerequisite for the United States to regain its stature as a first-class power in the world economy is a sharp reduction in programs benefiting older Americans. From the late 1970s until little more than a year ago, there were many complaints that Social Security's Old Age and Survivors Insurance trust fund would be continually on the verge of "going broke," thereby posing an intolerable tax burden for American workers and their employers. Now that projections show substantial trust fund surpluses for the decades ahead, economists have begun analyzing and debating whether such surpluses will adversely affect the performance of the American economy.[30, 31]

Perhaps the most serious scapegoating of the aged—in terms of vulnerability of older persons and, possibly, of all persons in our society—has been with respect to health care. A widespread concern about escalating health care costs has somehow been refocused from the health care providers, suppliers, administrators, and insurers—the parties responsible for setting the prices of care—to the elderly patients for whom health care is provided.

Older persons account for one-third of our annual health care expenditures.[32] Because the elderly population is growing, absolutely and proportionately, health care costs for older persons have been depicted as an unsustainable burden, or as some have put it, "a great fiscal black hole"[33] that will absorb an unlimited amount of our national resources.

This scapegoating of the aged for health care costs has developed to the point that proposals have been put forward to deny life-saving health care to older persons. The substantial attention that such proposals have received in serious public forums may be the clearest signal that American public policy toward health care of the aging is approaching an important crossroads.

Health care in the United States has always been rationed informally on the basis of availability of resources, and the individual conditions and characteristics of patients. But proposals for official policies that would deny care categorically, on the basis of membership in a demographically identified group, are a substantial departure from existing practices and philosophies.

The suggestion that health care should be rationed on the basis of old age began to develop, through implication, in 1983. In a speech to the Health Insurance Association of America, economist Alan Greenspan, now chairman of the Federal Reserve Board, stated that 30 percent of Medicare is annually expended on 5 to 6 percent of Medicare eligibles who die within the year. He pointedly asked whether it is worth it.[34]

In 1984, the then Governor of Colorado, Richard Lamm, was widely quoted as stating that older persons "have a duty to die and get out of the way."[35] Although Lamm subsequently retracted this specific statement, he has traveled throughout the nation since leaving office, delivering this same message in somewhat more delicately worded fashions.[36]

During the past few years this issue has spread to a number of forums. Philosophers have been generating principles of equity to undergird "justice between age groups" in the provision of health care.[37] Conferences and books have explicitly addressed the issue "Should Health Care Be Rationed By Age?"[38]

Late in 1987 this theme reached new heights of legitimacy with the publication of a widely reviewed book by Daniel Callahan, a well-known medical ethicist. The book, entitled *Setting Limits: Medical Goals in an Aging Society*, proposes that older persons should be denied life-saving health care if they are in their late seventies or early eighties" and/or have "lived out a natural life span."[39]

The significance of this book lies in the extraordinary attention it has received. It has been reviewed in national magazines, *The New York Times*, *The Washington Post*, *The Wall Street Journal*, and just about every relevant professional and scholarly journal and newsletter. It appears that proposals for national policies to ration health care of older persons are an acceptable topic for public discussion in contemporary America.

Callahan views older Americans as "a new social threat" and a "demographic, economic, and medical avalanche . . . that could ultimately (and perhaps already) do great harm."[40] His remedy for this threat is to use "age as a specific criterion for the allocation and limitation of health care."[41] He justifies his proposal by emphasizing the burdensome costs of health care for older persons, and by arguing that "the meaning and significance of life for the elderly themselves is best founded on a sense of limits to health care."[42]

Older persons, in addition to being numerous and requiring large amounts of health care, are regarded by Callahan as selfish. He blames their selfishness on "mainline" advocates for the aged who have stressed for over two decades the rights and entitlements of the elderly. He accuses advocates of brainwashing older persons to believe that the process of aging is utterly diverse, that the aged are varied (like any other age group), and that old age is a time of renewed vigor, growth, self-discovery, and contributions to the community.

Although Callahan presents his case for rationing in a judicious style with a veneer of scholarly balance, his arguments are seriously flawed because they are often incomplete, imbalanced, illogical, and internally contradictory.[43] Two flaws, in particular, should be highlighted because of their very serious moral implications.

One flaw is that Callahan does not even attempt to convey how much money would be saved if his proposal were implemented. If the costs of health care for older persons are an unsustainable burden for our society, to what extent would that burden be relieved by old-age-based rationing? Previous calculations have suggested that even if all the funds that are spent on very high-cost Medicare patients who die within a year were not expended, the savings would be negligible.[44]

In 1987, the year Callahan's book was published, we spent over $500 billion on health care in the United States, and $170 billion of that was on persons aged 65 and older. If Callahan's proposal had been implemented, would the aggregate savings have been $1 billion, $5 billion, $25 billion? Assuming that any amount of money could justify his proposal, shouldn't he provide some basis for judging whether it is worth it? Otherwise we are left with what amounts to a naked attack on the lives of older persons.

The other major flaw is Callahan's total neglect of the moral implications of singling out any group of Americans as not worthy of life-extending care. What impact would such a policy have on the moral fabric of American society? What group might be singled out next as undesirable, burdensome, and costly? If the aged can become vulnerable through scapegoating, who among us is next in line? Are the economic burdens of health care costs greater than the moral burdens of officially denying health care to a demographically defined category of citizens?

In view of such flaws, the very fact that a proposal such as Callahan's has been put forward and treated seriously in the mainstream of American public discourse indicates a new vulnerability for the aged in American public opinion. This proposal and the attention it has received may not represent the climax of the process through which the aged have become a scapegoat.

In addition to a continuing flow of media stereotypes of the old, the activities of a new organization established to propound issues of "intergenerational equity"—Americans for Generational Equity (AGE)—appear to have solid financial backing from the corporate sector as well as from selected members of Congress.[45] Each year AGE holds several conferences on issues of generational equity throughout the nation. From its Washington office it publishes and disseminates *The Generational Journal*.

Central to AGE's credo is the proposition that the large aggregate of public transfers of income and other benefits to today's cohorts of older persons, financed through unfairly burdensome taxes on the contemporary labor force, are unlikely to be available in the future as old age benefits (e.g., Social Security and Medicare) when the present cohort of workers becomes elderly retirees.[46] Moreover, AGE contrasts the relatively prosperous circumstances of the elderly with those of other groups such as disadvantaged children and an estimated 37 million Americans who lack health insurance. Every indication suggests that this organization will likely persist in adding to the rhetoric that pits the young and the middle-aged against an artificially homogenized group of older Americans, as exemplified by the title of one of AGE's recent conferences—"Children at Risk: Who Will Support Our Aging Society?"

The Politics of Older Persons and Aging-Based Organizations

To what extent have the politics of older persons and old-age–based organizations contributed to the present climate in which the aged have emerged as scapegoat? Is the power of the aging sufficient to reverse this trend?

After all, it is conventional wisdom in the media,[47] as well as among scholars who would make a scapegoat of the aged,[48] that older persons are one of the most powerful constituencies in American politics. A brief examination of the aging in American politics will indicate, however, that this bit of conventional wisdom, as is the case with much conventional wisdom, is very oversimplified.

VOTING BEHAVIOR OF OLDER PERSONS

Voting is one of the main sources of power available to mass constituencies in the American political system. Persons aged 65 and older do constitute a large bloc of participating voters. They have comprised from 16.7 to 21 percent of those who have actually voted in national elections during the 1980s.[49] And this percentage range is likely to become elevated in the next four decades because of projected increases in the proportion of older Americans.

But older persons do not vote in a monolithic bloc, any more than middle-aged persons or younger persons do. Consequently, the aged do not wield power as a single-issue voting constituency.

As Tables 3-1 and 3-2 from recent presidential and congressional elections should make clear, election exit polls have shown repeatedly that the votes of older persons distribute among candidates in about the same proportions as the votes of other age groupings of citizens. Although men and women can be seen to have distributed their votes differently, persons in the age categories of 30 to 44, 45 to 59, and 60 years of age and older cast their ballots in these elections in a similar fashion. Examination of properly sampled exit polls from other national elections shows the same patterns of distribution, by age categories.

These data should not be surprising since there is no sound reason to expect that a cohort of persons would suddenly become homogenized in its political behavior when it reaches the "old age"

Table 3-1. Nationwide Vote Distribution, by Age Group and Sex in Recent Elections for U.S. President

	1980			1984		1988	
	Reagan	Carter	Anderson	Reagan	Mondale	Bush	Dukakis
Percentage of all voters	51%	41%	7%	59%	41%	53%	45%
Percentage of men							
All ages	55	36	7	62	37	57	41
18–29 years old	47	39	11	61	37	55	43
30–44 years old	59	31	4	62	37	58	40
44–59 years old	60	34	5	63	36	62	36
60 years and older	56	40	3	62	37	53	46
Percentage of women							
All ages	47	45	7	56	44	50	49
18–29 years old	39	49	10	55	45	49	50
30–44 years old	50	41	8	54	46	50	49
44–59 years old	50	44	5	58	41	52	48
60 years and older	52	43	4	64	35	48	52
Percentage of adults							
18–29 years old	43	44	11	58	41	52	47
30–44 years old	54	36	8	58	42	54	45
44–59 years old	55	39	5	60	39	57	42
60 years and older	54	41	4	63	36	50	49

SOURCES: 1980, 1984, and 1988 nationwide exit polls conducted by *The New York Times*/CBS News, published in *The New York Times*, November 9, 1980; November 9, 1984; and November 10, 1988.

Table 3-2. Nationwide Vote Distribution, by Age Group in Recent Elections for U.S. House of Representatives

	1982		1984		1986	
	Democrat	Republican	Democrat	Republican	Democrat	Republican
Percentage of all voters	57%	43%	51%	49%	52%	48%
Percentage of men						
18–29 years old	60	40	47	53	48	52
30–44 years old	52	48	52	48	52	48
44–59 years old	54	46	47	53	50	50
60 years and older	56	44	46	54	51	49
Percentage of women						
18–29 years old	58	42	56	44	54	46
30–44 years old	57	43	56	44	52	48
44–59 years old	58	42	52	48	58	42
60 years and older	60	40	51	49	53	47
Percentage of adults						
18–29 years old	59	41	51	49	51	49
30–44 years old	54	46	54	46	52	48
44–59 years old	56	44	50	50	54	46
60 years and older	58	42	48	52	52	48

SOURCE: 1982, 1984, and 1986 nationwide exit polls conducted by *The New York Times*/CBS News, published in *The New York Times*, November 6, 1986, p. 15Y.

category. Diversity among older persons may be at least as great with respect to political attitudes and behavior as it is in relation to economic, social, and other characteristics.[50]

The very assumption that mass groupings of the American citizenry vote primarily on the basis of self-interested responses to single issues is, in itself, problematic. Candidates, not issues, run for office. In the context of choosing between candidates, a voter's response to any one issue is part of an overall response to a variety of issues in a campaign, and to many other stimuli that may have little to do with specific issues, or the presumed "self-interest" that might be implied by a single issue.[51]

Moreover, within a heterogeneous group such as older persons, self-interested responses to any single issue are likely to vary substantially. The best available studies show that even in the context of a state or local referendum that presents a specific issue for balloting—such as propositions to cap local property taxes or to finance public schools—old age is not a statistically significant variable associated with the distribution of votes.[52]

But don't politicians behave as if older persons vote as a bloc in response to issues? Aren't they terrorized by so-called senior power? The answer is not clear, judging from a case study of a presidential election campaign in which relatively negligible financial resources and efforts were expended on wooing older voters.[53]

It is certainly evident that no politician goes out of his or her way to offend the aged. On the other hand, there have been numerous cases in recent years, enumerated below, when Congress has enacted legislation that has adversely affected the presumed interests of the aged.

AGING-BASED INTEREST GROUPS

Only limited power is available to "The Gray Lobby,"[54] which consists of the aging-based mass membership interest groups such as the American Association of Retired Persons (AARP) and the National Council of Senior Citizens (NCSC), as well as dozens of other professional and business organizations "representing" older persons. As implied by the preceding discussion of electoral behavior, such organizations have not been able to cohere or even to shift marginally the votes of older persons. While AARP claims more than

28 million members, for example, it does not control or demonstrably influence their votes.[55] In the 1980 presidential campaign, the leaders of a number of major aging-based organizations vigorously endorsed President Carter in his bid for re-election. Nonetheless, a majority of older persons voted for his opponent, Ronald Reagan, and in the same proportion as voters in younger age groupings (see Table 3-1).

Experience in other modern democratic states, such as Great Britain and Sweden, has been comparable. Attempts to organize the votes of older persons to affect the fate of a particular candidate, party, or proposition have not been notably successful.[56]

Organized demands of older persons have had little to do with the enactment and amendment of the major old-age policies such as Social Security and Medicare. Rather, such actions have been largely attributable to the initiatives of public officials in the White House, Congress, and the bureaucracy who have focused on their own agendas for social and economic policy.[57–61] The impact of old-age–based interest groups has been largely confined to relatively minor policies, enacted from the mid-1960s to the mid-1970s, that have distributed benefits to professionals and practitioners in the field of aging rather than directly to older persons themselves.[62–64]

Some forms of power, however, are available to old-age interest groups. In the classic pattern of American interest-group politics, public officials find it both useful and incumbent upon themselves to invite such organizations to participate in policy activities. In this way, public officials are provided with a ready means of having been "in touch" symbolically with millions of constituents, thereby legitimizing subsequent policy actions and inactions. A brief meeting with the leaders of these organizations can enable an official to claim that he or she has duly obtained the represented views of a mass constituency.

The legitimacy that old-age organizations have for participating in interest group politics gives them several forms of power.

First, they have easy informal access to public officials: members of Congress and their staffs; career bureaucrats; appointed officials; and occasionally to the White House. They can put forth their own proposals—regarding Medicare, nursing home regulations, Social Security, and a variety of other matters—and work to block the proposals of others. To be sure, their audiences or targets may be unresponsive in subsequent policy decisions. But access provides some measure of opportunity.

Second, their legitimacy enables them to obtain public platforms in the national media, at congressional hearings, and in national conferences and commissions dealing with old age, health, and a variety of subjects relevant to policies affecting aging. From these platforms the old-age organizations can exercise power by initiating and framing issues for public debate, and responding to issues raised by others.

A third form of power available to these groups might be termed "the electoral bluff." Although these organizations have not demonstrated a capacity to swing a decisive bloc of older voters, incumbent members of Congress are hardly inclined to risk upsetting the existing distribution of votes that puts them and keeps them in office. Few politicians want to call the bluff of the aged or any other latent mass constituency if it is possible to avoid doing so. In fact, the image of "senior power" is frequently invoked by politicians when—for one reason or another—they desire an excuse for doing nothing or for not differentiating themselves from their colleagues and electoral opponents.

These forms of power, while minor when compared with the power available to organizations that are based on major economic interests, may have some limited impact. Today, as policies affecting old age have become prominent on the agenda of domestic policy issues, the old-age interest organizations seem to have become one of what political scientist Heclo[65] terms "anti-redistributive veto forces" in American politics. The limited power these organizations have available to them is being applied in a defensive effort to maintain the existing distribution of benefits and privileges among older persons, as well as among the many professional and practitioner interests that have emerged and flourished in relation to the growth of the elderly population.

But despite such efforts by old-age interest groups, a number of public policy decisions that are conventionally perceived as adverse to the self-interest of older persons proved to be politically feasible in the 1980s through changes in Medicare, Social Security, and other programs. Medicare deductibles, co-payments, and Part B premiums have increased continuously. Old Age Insurance (OAI) benefits have been made subject to taxation. The legislated formula for Cost-Of-Living Adjustments (COLAs) to OAI benefits has been rendered less generous. The Omnibus Reconciliation Act of 1981 narrowed five benefit and eligibility provisions of Social Security, which had a direct adverse effect on OAI recipients. And The Tax Reform Act of 1986 eliminated the extra personal exemption that all persons 65 years of age and older had been receiving in filing their federal income tax returns.

These changes are relatively minor, of course, in comparison to drastic changes in old age programs—such as totally dismantling Social Security—proposed by some politicians and discussed by policy analysts in recent years. And the defensive efforts of old-age interest groups, through the limited forms of power available to them, may have had some impact in "containing the damage." But the relatively minor character of these changes is just as likely attributable to ways in which the underlying American penchants for political incrementalism and pragmatism are being expressed by Congress in response to the policy challenges of an aging society.[66, 67]

Congressional Trends

If the future of public policy toward older persons will not be controlled strongly by a self-interested constituency of the aging, what trends can be identified in congressional activity as the next White House Conference on Aging draws near? Does Congress show signs of being caught up in the hostile atmosphere through which the aged have emerged as a scapegoat? Or are there signs that it will undertake policies that focus more explicitly than in the past on the diversity of older Americans? What are the prospects for those among the aged who still remain highly disadvantaged?

Congress has shown no inclination to make Draconian cuts in Social Security, Medicare, and other programs for the aged that have become well-established features of American life, despite its preoccupations with reducing the federal deficit. To be sure, some members of Congress are among the founding members of Americans for Generational Equity, and have recruited former Governor Lamm, demographer Preston, biomedical ethicist Callahan, and others of a like mind. But they have yet to inject into the legislative process their views that the so-called intergenerational inequities represented by programs benefiting the aging should be redressed through drastic policy changes. So far they have confined their efforts to conferences, speeches, and publications.

To the contrary, as the 1980s drew to a close Congress enacted the first major expansion of benefits to older persons since 1972 when Social Security benefits were markedly elevated and indexed for inflation. Through the Medicare Catastrophic Coverage Act of 1988, public insurance was provided to cap older persons' obligations to pay for hospital bills; limit (though not absolutely cap) their payments to physicians; reimburse outpatient prescription drug charges (after a deductible has been met); and provide some elements of long-term care (expanded coverage for care in skilled-nursing facilities, hospices, and at home). The Congressional Budget Office has estimated the cost of these new benefits (and administration of them) for fiscal years 1989 through 1993 at $30.8 billion.

Notable, in two respects, is the manner in which these new benefits are financed. First, the benefits are financed solely by a tax on the elderly through both Medicare Part A and Part B premiums, rather than through the Federal Insurance Contribution Act payroll tax (which helps to fund Medicare Part A benefits) or general revenues. Part B premiums had been increased many times before. But the new benefits provide coverage of services that have been traditionally clustered with both Part A and Part B. From all accounts the White House and congressional leaders self-consciously determined that the new benefits would be "self financed," that is, paid for wholly by the elderly themselves.[68]

Second, and perhaps more notable, is that the new Part A premiums were levied as a semiprogressive tax, with a ceiling on income-determined tax liability. Congress rejected the administration's initial proposal for a flat, regressive premium. Instead it established an across-the-board small payment for all Part B participants, and in addition levied Part A taxes on a sliding scale in relation to enrollees' incomes. It financed 37 percent of the new benefits by adding $4 a month to the Part B premium to be paid by every enrollee, and raised the remaining 63 percent of revenues through a "supplemental" premium or Part A tax to be paid by approximately 40 percent of participants on the basis of their federal income tax liability. In 1989, each Medicare enrollee paid $22.50 a year for every $150 of income tax liability, up to a limit of $800 per individual and $1,600 per couple.

This semiprogressive financing mechanism reflected what was, perhaps, the main trend in policy toward the aging in the 1980s: an acknowledgment that "the elderly" are a diverse group, and that old age is not an accurate marker of economic status. The Social Security Reform Act of 1983 began this trend by taxing Social Security benefits for recipients in higher income brackets. The Tax Reform Act of 1986, even as it eliminated the extra personal exemption that had been available categorically to all persons 65 years and older when filing their federal income tax, provided tax credits to very low-income older persons on a sliding scale. And the Older Americans Act programs of supportive and social services have been evolving toward sliding fee scales. The Medicare Catastrophic Coverage Act of 1988 continued this trend.

The principle of treating older persons through public policy as if they were all the same seems to be weakening as a greater sensitivity to the diverse circumstances of older persons is being legislatively expressed. But the primary emphasis of this sensitivity has been on the differing capacities of older persons to help finance public programs. Little has been done in recent years to focus on seriously ameliorating the situations of those among the aged who remain extremely disadvantaged.

Since 1988 there has been a plethora of congressional bills for public long-term care insurance. These bills appeared to arise primarily from a middle-class concern about "spending down" assets in the process of becoming eligible for Medicaid, the welfare program that provides public reimbursement for nursing home care and some elements of home health care. Little attention was being paid to those who have nothing to spend down to begin with.

Reforming old age policies to focus effective help to disadvantaged subgroups is not a difficult technical problem. Proposals for changing OAI and SSI so as to target income-maintenance policies to the most economically vulnerable elderly, for example, have been discussed for years.[69–72] Practicable proposals for progressively redistributing the burdens and benefits of Medicare have been widely publicized.[73] Innumerable legislative and administrative measures are feasible for decisively targeting the relatively small amount of service resources available under Title III of the Older Americans Act to minorities and/or the economically needy.[74]

But such proposals have not been strongly supported politically, either by Congress or by the major organizations in the field of aging. For now, Congress seems to be undertaking a highly pragmatic and incremental approach toward programs on aging, with some heightened sense of the diverse economic situations of older persons. As the next White House Conference on Aging approaches, what might be the source of a new impetus for policies that focus on the most disadvantaged subgroups among the aged?

The Prospects for Diversity in Policies Toward the Aging

It should be evident from our earlier discussion of the politics of aging that the symbolic political legitimacy available to organized groups of older persons is their primary source of power. How can this power be applied for engendering public policies that focus on ameliorating the conditions experienced by the most disadvantaged aged?

The primary avenue available is through the politics of issue framing or, as it has been termed by political scientists, "agenda building."[75] This political strategy played a significant role in the early 1970s in establishing the National Institute on Aging,[76] and has been used effectively by Americans for Generational Equity in shaping current public discourse concerning policies on aging.[77]

While lay leaders and professionals concerned with severely disadvantaged older Americans could, in principle, set a public agenda by themselves, their chances would be greatly enhanced if they could harness the symbolic legitimacy of AARP and other old-age-based interest groups. Mobilizing the aging-based interest groups for this purpose, however, is not a simple challenge.

Some years ago the president of the American Coalition of Citizens with Disabilities expressed the hope that a coalition of the organized constituencies of older persons and the disabled might become a powerful force in American politics.[78] However, there has been no sign of such a movement since then. Indeed, the evidence and analysis in a case study of the politics involved in enactment of a long-term care bill in California[79] suggests that organized groups of the aged and disabled are more likely to compete with each other than to form an effective coalition.

To be sure, some of the so-called aging advocacy organizations are highly focused on subgroups within the older population.

The Villers Foundation, a small organization without a mass membership constituency, has a primary mission to focus on the plight of the poor and vulnerable elderly.[80] The Older Womens' League (OWL), is especially concerned with the economic issues confronting aging women. And specific organizations have been organized to advocate for the Asian and Pacific elderly, black elderly, Hispanic elderly, gay elderly, Native American elderly, rural elderly, and a variety of other subgroups. Separately, such organizations have a narrow range of symbolic legitimacy, speaking for constituencies that are viewed by politicians as relatively small.

Some of these groups—together with AARP, the American Association of Homes for the Aging, the Gerontological Society of America, the National Council on the Aging, the National Council of Senior Citizens, and others—are members of a larger coalition known as the Leadership Council of Organizations in Aging. But in the context of such a broad coalition, highly focused goals for specific subgroups naturally tend to become diluted. Perhaps the main function of the Leadership Council is that it provides Congress and other public officials with a convenient mechanism for symbolically receiving the homogenized views of dozens of organized constituencies through one representative, at one hearing or sitting.

In the case of the largest mass-membership organization, AARP, the very size of its membership—more than 28 million members—suggests that an agenda focusing on diversity among the aged may be impracticable for the organization. AARP does undertake and fund excellent periodic studies that focus on disadvantaged groups within the older population.[81] But a major political campaign focused on the needs of distinct subgroups of older persons might risk some membership loss to this organization, which is as large and diverse as the entire American population of persons aged 65 and older (although it should be noted that AARP membership begins at 50 years of age).

Moreover, the membership incentives that have maintained AARP to date have not been predominantly purposive or social-change oriented, especially with respect to improving the lot of disadvantaged subgroups of the elderly. The organization's drug, insurance, investment, and travel programs; its newsletter and magazines; the sociability and provision of information at its local chapter meetings; its leaders' accounts of dramatic meetings with politicians and recitations of issues facing the aged—these benefits have, up to now, seemed to provide members with adequate incentives for paying their annual membership dues.

Nonetheless, AARP may represent the best hope for a source of power that can effectively refocus the agenda of policies on aging to help the most disadvantaged older populations. Even though numbers do not necessarily equate with power, the American political system's enchantment with interest groups[82] lends AARP extraordinary political legitimacy since it is the largest interest group in the United States today.[83] And AARP may well choose to change its focus, particularly under the pressure of a political climate in which the aged are becoming a scapegoat for an ever-increasing roster of problems in American society.

Whether AARP or other entities and persons take leadership in framing issues for the 1990s, what might their strategies be? As issues of intergenerational equity began to occupy the agenda of polices on aging in the late 1980s, a variety of responses emerged.

One approach has been to argue that public benefits to older persons also are of value to persons of all ages through "ties that bind," particularly in a family context.[84] In a similar vein, it has been argued that issues of intergenerational equity can be defused and diffused through new public policies providing benefits that can be shared by persons of all ages,[85] and that programs based on age should be "played down" rather than "played up."[86] Another suggestion has been that old-age advocacy organizations—to demonstrate that they are not selfish—should form coalitions with other interest groups.[87] And still another approach has been to argue that issues of intergenerational equity are spurious, masking inequities among persons of all ages.[88]

Whatever strategy is employed, policies for eliminating the problems of the most severely disadvantaged aged will probably not emerge unless the special place that older persons have had in American health and welfare policy gives way to a broader focus on vulnerable persons of all ages. Such a focus would require an ideological consensus that our government should provide effective help to all persons who are not in a position to help themselves, regardless of age.

Ironically, the development of such a broadened American welfare consensus could be fostered through a preoccupation with the problems of old age and an understanding of the life-course experiences that lead to them. The persons who are most vulnerable in childhood and throughout their working years are the ones most likely to be vulnerable in old age, if they live that long.

More than twenty years ago President Lyndon B. Johnson presented a very open-ended charge to a White House Task Force on Older Americans: "What are the most important things that can be done for the well-being of the most older Americans?" The task force members well understood that vulnerability in old age is the product of a life course of experiences. Their priority statement to the president was that "economic and social opportunities for current generations of the young and middle-aged are the most effective measures for ensuring opportunities for future generations of older Americans."[89] Such a perspective on our common human vulnerability will need to be widely accepted before American public policy toward the aging and other constituencies develops a priority focus on helping our most vulnerable citizens.

Notes

1. Tolchin, M. "New health insurance plan provokes outcry over costs." *The New York Times*, November 2, 1988, p. 1.
2. "Correction: Two Plans for 1990." *The New York Times*, February 14, 1989.
3. Neugarten, B.L. "The old and the young in modern societies." *American Behavioral Scientist*, 14 (1970): 13–24.
4. Kutza, E.A. *The Benefits of Old Age*. Chicago: University of Chicago Press, 1981.
5. Estes, C.L. *The Aging Enterprise*. San Francisco: Jossey-Bass Publishers, 1979.
6. Myles, J.F. "Conflict, crisis, and the future of old age security." *Milbank Memorial Fund Quarterly/Health and Society* 61 (1983): 462–472.
7. Marmor, T.R. *The Politics of Medicare*. London: Routledge & Kegan Paul, 1970.
8. U.S. Senate Special Committee on Aging. *Developments in Aging: 1987—Volume I*. Washington, D.C.: U.S. Government Printing Office, 1988.
9. Clark, R.L. Income maintenance policies in the United States. In R.H. Binstock and L.K. George (Eds.) *Handbook of Aging and The Social Sciences*, 3rd ed. San Diego, Calif.: Academic Press, in press.
10. U.S. Senate Committee on Aging.
11. Kutza, *Benefits of Old Age*.
12. Nelson, G. "Social class and public policy for the elderly." *Social Service Review* 56 (1982): 85–107.

13. Crystal, S. *America's Old Age Crisis: Public Policy and the Two Worlds of Aging*, revised ed. New York: Basic Books, 1984.

14. U.S. Senate Committee on Aging, p. 6.

15. Smeeding, T.M. Economic status of the elderly. In R.H. Binstock and L.K. George (Eds.) *Handbook of Aging and the Social Sciences*, 3rd ed. San Diego, Calif.: Academic Press, in press.

16. U.S. Senate Committee on Aging, pp. 6–7.

17. Schulz, J.H. *The Economics of Aging*, 4th ed. Dover, Mass.: Auburn Publishing House Company, 1988.

18. Social Security in Review. *Social Security Bulletin* 51, 7 (1988): 3.

19. Schulz, J.H., and T.D. Leavitt, *Time to Reform the SSI Asset Test?* Washington, D.C.: American Association of Retired Persons, 1988.

20. U.S. Senate Committee on Aging.

21. Commonwealth Fund Commission on Elderly People Living Alone. *Old, Alone and Poor: A Plan for Reducing Poverty Among Elderly People Living Alone*. Baltimore: Commonwealth Fund Commission on Elderly People Living Alone, 1987.

22. Zedlewski, S.R. and J.A. Meyer. *Toward Ending Poverty Among the Elderly and Disabled: Policy and Financing Options*. Washington, D.C.: The Urban Institute, 1987.

23. Binstock, R.H. "The aged as scapegoat." *The Gerontologist* 23 (1983): 136–143.

24. Gibbs, N.R. "Grays on the go." *Time* 131, 8, (1988): 66–75.

25. Fairlie, H. "Talkin' 'bout my generation." *The New Republic* 198, 13, (1988): 19–22.

26. Allport, G.W. *ABC's of Scapegoating*. New York: Anti-Defamation League of B'nai B'rith, 1959, pp. 13–14.

27. Preston, S.H. "Children and the elderly in the U.S." *Scientific American* 251, 6 (1984) 44–49.

28. Carballo, M. Extra votes for parents? *The Boston Globe*, December 17, 1981, p. 35.

29. Peterson, P. "The morning after." *The Atlantic* 260, (1987): 43–69.

30. Kilborn, P.T. "New issue on budget horizon: What to do about surpluses." *The New York Times*, April 2, 1988, p. 1.

31. Munnell, A.H. and L.E. Blais. "Do we want large social security surpluses?" *The Generational Journal* 1, 1 (1988): 21–36.

32. U.S. Senate Committee on Aging, p. 12.

33. Callahan, D. *Setting Limits: Medical Goals for an Aging Society*. New York: Simon and Schuster, 1987, p. 16.

34. Schulte, J. "Terminal patients deplete Medicare, Greenspan says." *Dallas Morning News*, April 26, 1983, p. 1.

35. Slater, W. "Latest Lamm remark angers the elderly." *Arizona Daily Star*, March 29, 1984, p. 1.

36. Lamm, R.D. A debate: Medicare in 2020. In *Medicare Reform and the Baby Boom Generation*, edited proceedings of the second annual conference of Americans for Generational Equity. Washington, D.C.: Americans for Generational Equity, April 30-May 1, 1987, pp. 77–88.

37. Daniels, N. *Am I My Parents' Keeper? An Essay on Justice Between the Young and the Old*. New York: Oxford University Press, 1988.

38. Smeeding, T.M., M.P. Battin, L.P. Francis and B.M. Landesman (Eds.) *Should Medical Care Be Rationed by Age?* Totowa, N.J.: Rowman & Littlefield, 1987.

39. Callahan, *Setting Limits*, p. 171.

40. Ibid., p. 20.

41. Ibid., p. 23.

42. Ibid., p. 116.

43. Binstock, R.H. and J. Kahana. "An essay on *Setting Limits*: *Medical Goals in an Aging Society*," by D. Callahan. *The Gerontologist* 28 (1988): 424–426.

44. Rowe, J.W. and R.H. Binstock. Aging reconsidered: emerging research and policy issues. In E. Ginzberg (Ed.) *Medicine and Society*: *Clinical Decisions and Societal Values*. Boulder, Colo.: Westview Press, 1987, pp. 96–113.

45. Quadagno, J. "Generational equity and the politics of class." Paper presented at the annual meeting of the American Sociological Association, Atlanta, Ga., 1988.

46. Longman, P. *Born to Pay*: *The New Politics of Aging in America*, Boston, Mass.: Houghton Mifflin, 1987.

47. Chakravarty, S.N. and K. Weisman. "Consuming our children?" *Forbes*, 142 (Nov. 14, 1988): 222–232.

48. Preston, "Children and the Elderly in the U.S."

49. U.S. Senate Committee on Aging, p. 11.

50. Hudson, R.H. and J. Strate. Aging and political systems. In R.H. Binstock and E. Shanas (Eds.) *Handbook of Aging and the Social Sciences*, 2nd ed. New York: Van Nostrand Reinhold, 1985, 551–585.

51. Simon, H.A. "Human nature in politics: The dialogue of psychology with political science." *American Political Science Review* 79 (1985): 293–304.

52. Chomitz, K.M. "Demographic influences on local public education expenditure: A review of econometric evidence." Paper prepared for workshop of the Committee on Population Projection, National Research Council, Woods Hole, Massachusetts, Sept. 5–7, 1985.

53. Reimer, Y. and R.H. Binstock. "Campaigning for the senior vote: A case study of Carter's 1976 campaign." *The Gerontologist* 18 (1978): 517–524.

54. Pratt, H.J. *The Gray Lobby*. Chicago: University of Chicago Press, 1976.

55. Jacobs, B. "Aging and politics." In R.H. Binstock and L.K. George (Eds.) *Handbook of Aging and the Social Sciences*, 3rd ed. San Diego, Calif.: Academic Press, in press.

56. Heclo, H. *Modern Social Politics in Britain and Sweden: From Relief to Income Maintenance*. New Haven, Conn.: Yale University Press, 1974.

57. Cohen, W.J. "Securing social security." *New Leader* 66 (1985): 5–8.

58. Cohen, W.J. "Reflections on the enactment of Medicare and Medicaid." *Health Care Financing Review*. Baltimore, Md.: U.S. Department of Health and Human Services, 1985. (Annual Suppl.), pp. 3–11.

59. Derthick, M. *Policymaking for Social Security*. Washington, D.C.: The Brookings Institution, 1979.

60. Iglehart, J.K. "Medicare's new benefits: "Catastrophic health insurance." *New England Journal of Medicine* 320 (1989): 329–336.

61. Light, P. *Artful work: The Politics of Social Security Reform*. New York: Random House, 1985.

62. Binstock, R.H. "Interest-group liberalism and the politics of aging." *The Gerontologist* 12 (1972): 265–280.

63. Estes, *The Aging Enterprise*.

64. Lockett, B.A. *Aging, Politics, and Research: Setting the Federal Agenda for Research on Aging*. New York: Springer Publishing Company, 1983.

65. Heclo, H. "The political foundations of anti-poverty policy." IRP Conference Paper on Poverty and Policy: Retrospect and Prospects. Madison, Wis.: Institute for Research on Poverty, 1984, pp. 6–8.

66. Heclo, H. Generational politics. In J.L. Palmer, T. Smeeding, and B.B. Torrey (Eds.) *The Vulnerable*. Washington, D.C.: The Urban Institute Press, 1988, pp. 381–442.

67. Binstock, R.H., M.A. Levin, and R. Weatherley. "Political dilemmas of social intervention." In R.H. Binstock and E. Shanas (Eds.) *Handbook of Aging and the Social Sciences*, 2nd ed. New York: Van Nostrand Reinhold, 1985, pp. 589–618.

68. Iglehart, "Medicare's new benefits."

69. Pechman, J.A., H.J. Aaron and M.K. Taussig. *Social Security: Perspectives for Reform*. Washington, D.C.: The Brookings Institution, 1968.

70. Cohen, W.J. and M. Friedman (1972). *Social Security: Universal or Selective?* Washington, D.C.: American Enterprise Institute, 1972.

71. Munnell, A.H. *The Future of Social Security*. Washington, D.C.: The Brookings Institution, 1977.

72. Commonwealth Fund Commission.

73. Blumenthal, D., M. Schlesinger and P.B. Drumheller, and The Harvard Medicare Project. "The future of Medicare." *New England Journal of Medicine* 314 (1986): 722–728.

74. Binstock, R.H., J. Grigsby, and T.D. Leavitt. *An analysis of "targeting" policy options under Title III of the Older Americans Act*. Waltham, Mass.: Working Paper No. 16 of the National Aging Policy Center on Income Maintenance, Brandeis University, 1983.

75. Elder, C.D. and R.W. Cobb. "Agenda building and the politics of aging." *Policy Studies Journal* 13 (1984): 115–130.

76. Lockett, *Aging, Politics, and Research*.

77. Quadagno, "Generational equity."

78. Rubenfeld, P. "Ageism and disabilityism: Double jeopardy." In S.J. Brody and G.E. Ruff (Eds.) *Aging and Rehabilitation: Advances in the State of the Art*. New York: Springer Publishing Company, 1986, pp. 323–328.

79. Torres-Gil, F. and J. Pynoos. "Long-term care policy and interest groups struggles." *The Gerontologist* 26 (1986): 488–495.

80. Villers Foundation. *Mission and Guidelines: Nurturing a Movement of Empowerment Among Elders*. Washington, D.C.: Villers Foundation, 1983.

81. Schulz and Leavitt, AARP.

82. Lowi, T.J. (1969). *The End of Liberalism*. New York: W.W. Norton & Co., 1969.

83. Jacobs, "Aging in politics."

84. Kingson, E.R., B.A. Hirshorn and J.M. Cornman. *Ties that Bind: The Interdependence of Generations*. Washington, D.C.: Seven Locks Press, 1986.

85. Wisensale, S.M. "Generational equity and intergenerational policies." *The Gerontologist* 28 (1988): 773–778.

86. Neugarten, B.L. and D.A. Neugarten. "Age in the aging society." *Daedalus* 115, (1986): 31–49.

87. Kingson, E.R. "Generational equity: an unexpected opportunity to broaden the politics of aging." *The Gerontologist* 28 (1988): 765–772.

88. Binstock, R.H. "The oldest-old: A fresh perspective or compassionate ageism revisited?" *Milbank Memorial Fund Quarterly/Health and Society* 63 (1985): 420–451.

89. President's Task Force on Older Americans. *Report of the President's Task Force on Older Americans*. Washington, D.C.: Executive Office of the President of the United States, 1968.

CHAPTER FOUR

Responding to Diversity: Is American Society Capable?

ELIZABETH ANN KUTZA

A social worker in a rural county sees a number of frail older persons who need personal assistance. While a state program can pay for such services, program rules require that payment be made only to formal agencies, of which there are none in the area. Why won't the state pay available family or neighbors to assist such older persons?

Mr. and Mrs. Smith are an elderly couple who have resided in their car for more than a year. Mr. Smith is hostile and abusive and spends their Social Security income on storing items he collects from alleys. Mrs. Smith is either demented or developmentally disabled. She has not been closely examined because her husband makes her stay in their junk- and lice-infested car. They refuse services and disappear if service providers threaten to intervene. Why can't the state take action to protect Mr. and Mrs. Smith?

A hospital worker in New Jersey wants to arrange home health care for an elderly patient who is soon to be discharged. But Medicaid will not cover the client. Were the client living ten miles away in the state of New York, a generous package of home care would be available. Why is there such variability in our social programs among states?

Anyone who works for an agency that provides a service to an older person, or who advocates on behalf of older persons, undoubtedly has encountered frustrations such as these. Why is it that policies so frequently seem unresponsive to the needs of individuals?

And why is it that public policymakers, that is, elected and appointed government officials, so often seem reluctant to expand social and health programs so as to make them more generous and humane? Other mature democracies have much more elaborate networks of universally available services than those found in the United States. The Canadian government, for example, provides national health insurance coverage for its citizens and yet manages to contain health care costs better than we do. Case finding and delivery of social services on a neighborhood level is not just a dream in Great Britain, but a reality. And in Scandinavia, a range of assisted housing options is available to aged and disabled persons within their own communities.

Critics of American social programs attribute these shortcomings to a lack of will on the part of elected officials, or even a mean-spiritedness. But a better explanation is found in our American heritage, a heritage that has shaped a unique political and economic context.

What follows is a primer that explains this context and explores its effect on the social and health programs that we develop and services we deliver. It is only by understanding this context that we can judge the extent to which our society can respond to an increasingly diverse older population.

The Government: What It Does Matters

It is now widely accepted that our government—federal, state, local—has an obligation to respond to the needs of older persons. The mere existence of a White House Conference on Aging attests to that acceptance. Advocates for the elderly today not only monitor the performance of public programs but also agitate for their expansion. Yet, this phenomenon is quite new.

Before this century, how one lived out one's old age was determined by personal, family, and community arrangements. Through the nineteenth century, America was still essentially a rural country, so one's old age was spent on the farm, contributing to the extent possible, surrounded by family, and supported when necessary by church and community. Government assistance was available, usually at the local level, but restricted to those older persons who had no other options.

With the dawn of the twentieth century, however, changing patterns of work and family life presented older persons with a less predictable future. Urbanization, industrialization, and economic recessions began to pull out from under the elderly their stable moorings of family and community. By the 1930s, a recognition of these changing social circumstances led to the passage of the Social Security Act and to the acceptance by government of its obligation to provide income assistance to all older persons.

Today, and in the future, how Americans will spend their old age is in large part shaped by the decisions made by government leaders and enacted through our public policies. But in order for advocates and service providers to explain what exists today and anticipate what will be feasible tomorrow, it is important to understand the context in which public policies are developed. Specifically, one must become familiar with the assumptions and values underlying America's political and economic systems, as well as their operation.

In What Do We Believe?

A well-known economist once observed,

> Contemporary American society is, in one sense, a split-level structure. Its political and social institutions provide universally distributed rights and privileges that proclaim the equality of all citizens. But its economic institutions rely on market-determined incomes that generate substantial disparities among citizens in living standards and material welfare. . . . The resulting mixture of equal rights and unequal incomes creates tensions between the political principles of democracy and the economic principles of capitalism.[1]

This tension between a drive toward political equality and an acceptance of economic inequality in many ways defines the American character and differentiates it from that of its European or North American cousins.

Unlike the European experience, with its history of feudalism and then monarchy, and the Canadian and Australian experiences, with colonial rule, the American political experience originated from a reaction to centralized authority and a desire to protect individual freedoms from government encroachment. While by 1601 the Poor Laws in Elizabethan England defined what role the government *should* play in the lives of its needy citizens, the framers of the American Constitution in 1789 specifically detailed what the government *should not do* vis-à-vis its citizens, needy or otherwise. Our Bill of Rights reflects a view of government as dangerous, not benign; as a threat to individual freedoms, not an aid to community solidarity; and as a power to be reined in, not a strength to be harnessed for good.

Our preoccupation with the individual—individual rights and individual possibilities—was a source of some interest to the Frenchman Alexis de Tocqueville when he visited the United States in 1830. He noted that egalitarianism was an overriding theme of American life and that our belief in equality "begets in man the desire of judging of everything for himself: it gives him, on all things, a taste for the tangible and the real, *a contempt for tradition and for forms*." De Tocqueville goes on to observe that "equality places men side by side, unconnected by any common tie, and predisposes them not to consider fellow creatures. It is difficult to draw a man out of his own circle to interest him in the destiny of the state, because he does not clearly understand what influence the destiny of the state can have upon his own lot."[2]

In contrast to the European society of his experience, with its class distinctions and strong centralized government, this visitor found an egalitarian society at once fascinating and disturbing. In his view, an emphasis on equality led to a reliance on self, no rules of interaction, no obligations expected or extended, value placed on one's own opinion, and an expectation that anyone can achieve success.

While de Tocqueville's observations on the American character may appear quaint in language, they remain current in substance. A more recent study of American cultural mores supports many of these earlier observations and affirms that individualism has marched inexorably through our history.[3]

Americans' lack of a collective sense of society and their ambivalence about government as a vehicle through which they can satisfy the collective good makes the United States a "reluctant welfare state."[4] While individual Americans can be personally generous in response to the needs of others, they are less eager to support generous social programs for an entire class of needy persons.

And it is this heritage that continues to influence the American character and explain why we, as a nation, have not adopted broad national programs in the area of income maintenance, health care, or long-term care. More important, it explains why we are not likely to adopt models from abroad, models that have been developed within a different heritage and set of cultural values.

Four Themes of Politics

As has been noted, our Founding Fathers were deeply suspicious of a centralized government. They worried about the tyranny that could be exercised by a powerful chief executive, and they feared the control a central government could exercise over the states. As a result, they designed a system in which power was highly fragmented and disbursed. Thus four themes are reflected in our political system—checks and balances among the three branches of government; democratic pluralism; states' rights; and individual rights. These themes directly affect our current programs for the elderly in several important ways.

Consider the difficulty we have had trying to develop a national long-term care policy. The "facts" make a strong case for a universal continuum-of-care system that responds to the social and medical needs of frail older persons.

First, demographics point to the broadening need for such a system. In particular, the numbers of "old old," those 85 and older, are growing. While not all persons this old are frail and in need of formal long-term care services, increased age does correlate with increased disability. The rate of needing help in at least one basic physical activity is substantially higher among people in the older-age categories. The rate for people 85 years of age and older (348 per 1,000) is even markedly higher than that for people 75 to 84 years of age (114 per 1,000).[5]

Second, more and more families are experiencing the personal and financial burdens brought about by the care needs of their aged relatives. Few elderly persons living in the community use formal services. Almost four-fifths of people aged 65 years and over, or approximately 21 million elderly individuals, do not use any community services.[6] Many of those who need care rely on their families. In the matter of formal long-term care services, federal and state governments today pay for about 47 percent; the remainder is the responsibility of older persons themselves or their families.[7]

Finally, benefits available to persons in need of long-term care are highly medicalized, primarily delivered within nursing homes, and vary from state to state. Thus, they do not reflect the assistance preferred by frail older persons and their families, nor do they represent a fair treatment of older persons who have similar needs.

Study after study has pointed to these "facts" and argued that good public policy would lead in the direction of a federally funded program with standardized benefits that would be universally available on the basis of need, not income or place of residence, and that would treat frail elderly individuals as persons in need of care, not patients in need of treatment. So why don't we have such a program? Because of the constraints imposed by our political structures and belief systems.

WHO'S IN CHARGE?

One advantage of a strong centralized government is its capacity for central planning and unified decisionmaking. Both of these advantages are lost in the U.S. system. Yet, an absence of central coordination and control, in theory, does have some advantages. First, having a number of decisionmakers involved in each policy choice should help prevent errors, since all must agree to a proposal before it can be enacted into law or made into an operating program. Also, the existence of several decisionmakers should permit greater innovation, at all levels of government. And, as intended, diffuse power reduces the capacity of one central government to run roughshod over the rights of citizens.

But in practice, this division of power—among the legislative, executive, and judicial branches—has some obvious negative impacts on public policies. In particular, the number of clearance points in the federal government alone makes initiating any policy difficult and makes preventing change relatively easy. It also makes it difficult to identify just which branch of government will be most influential in the shaping of a particular policy.

Social Security provides us with a case in point. In analyzing how the Social Security program came to be what it is, Derthick highlights the fact that it was the executive branch of government, not elected officials in the legislative branch, that gave shape to the program.[8] Congress deferred to the "experts" within the executive branch on this technically complex idea, thus allowing these same experts to present their preferred proposals in ways that "enhanced acceptability to the public in general, the public's elected representatives, and diverse private interests." These executives designed the program and minimized its costs to Congress, and in the words of Derthick, they "also minimized the other sorts of costs that are normally associated with public policymaking, including especially the psychological and political costs associated with innovation, uncertainty, and disagreement." Their proposals were invariably presented as extensions of more familiar programs.

In addition to influencing the shape of public programs, administrative agency personnel, when they wish to, can impede policy change or block it entirely. Almost every elected official has had the experience of fighting the delaying tactics of nominal subordinates who disagree with a policy choice and who merely wait for the next election or cabinet shake-up to see whether someone whose policy ideas they prefer will come into office. The very permanence of these civil servants and their command of both the technical issues and the procedural machinery give the agencies of the public bureaucracy a great deal more power over public programs than one would assume from reading the formal descriptions of government institutions.

The committee structure in Congress provides another illustration of how the dispersion of power may impede sensible program development.

Most legislative activity proceeds through committees, and then must be ratified by the whole legislative body and signed by the chief executive officer, that is , the President. Committees are divided into substantive areas of jurisdiction, for example, veterans' affairs, education and labor, commerce. Programs that serve older persons hence do not fall under the jurisdiction of one committee, but of several. Jurisdictional authority by program is displayed below:

Table 4-1. Committee Jurisdiction for Programs Affecting the Elderly

Program	Senate Committee	House Committee
Food stamps	Agriculture, Nutrition, Forestry	Agriculture
Housing	Banking, Housing, Urban Affairs	Banking, Finance, Urban Affairs
Older Americans Act/ *NIA*	Labor & Human Resources	Education & Labor
Medicaid	Finance	Energy/Commerce
Age discrimination	Judiciary	Judiciary
Transportation	Commerce/Science/ Transportation	Public Works/ Transportation
Veterans	Veterans Affairs	Veterans Affairs
SSA, SSI, Medicare	Finance	Ways & Means

The implications of these jurisdictional divisions can be seen by returning to our long-term care example. (For simplicity, we will look at only one chamber in Congress, the Senate.)

The major federal program that pays for long-term care services is the Medical Assistance or Medicaid program. Through federal Medicaid grants, states are required to provide skilled medical services, and allowed to provide intermediate care nursing home services to those who qualify by virtue of functional disability and low income. In 1985, one-third of all Medicaid dollars went for nursing home care, accounting for 42 percent of our nation's nursing home care bills.[9] While some Medicaid dollars support community-based long-term care, most support institutional care. Jurisdiction for the Medicaid program rests with the Senate Finance Committee.

In recent years, community-based long-term care services of a more social nature—that is, homemaker, chore, legal assistance, nutrition—have been supported by the budget of another federal grant program, the Older Americans Act. Consideration of any expansion of, or amendment to, the Older Americans Act falls under the jurisdiction of another committee, Labor and Human Resources.

Part of the difficulty we have had in developing a long-term care system that is less medically focused is directly attributable to this jurisdictional split. Finance Committee members see Medicaid as a medical assistance program. It should pay for services of health professionals—doctors, nurses, physical therapists. Since homemakers and chore workers are not health professionals, paying them is more suspect. Social models of intervention are not seen as an appropriate focus of the Medicaid program by these legislators. They believe that social models should remain within the social programs.

Unfortunately, this attitude perpetuates the historic imbalance that we see in the funding of medically focused versus socially focused long-term care services. In the 1990 fiscal year budget, for example, $37.4 billion federal Medicaid dollars are expected to be spent (matched by a roughly equal number of state dollars), approximately one-third of which will pay our country's nursing home bill. Contrast this to the $800 million budgeted for the Older Americans Act in this same fiscal year.[10]

In fact, the only way that states have been able to insert community-based social services into the long-term care continuum has been through requesting a waiver of existing Medicaid regulations. Thus, such services are allowed through exception, not as a matter of planned policy choice. And it is likely that these various committee territorial and jurisdictional boundary prerogatives will continue to stand in the way of developing the long-term care system that advocates for the elderly and the elderly themselves prefer.

It becomes clear, then, that the separation of power that is built into our policymaking system can lead to confusion as to who's in charge, and can lead to obstacles when innovations are desired.

STAKING A CLAIM IN THE SYSTEM

Democratic pluralism is another particular theme of our political system that influences what the government does for older persons. American policies and programs are shaped by the pulling and tugging of special interests. There is a belief in this country, dating back to James Madison's statement of political philosophy in *The Federalist Papers*, that the multiplicity of interests that characterize a free society will provide security for civil rights. Madison wrote: "Whilst all authority in (the United States) will be derived from and dependent on the society, the society itself will be broken into so many parts, interests and classes of citizens, that the rights of individuals, or of the minority, will be in little danger from interested combinations of the majority."[11]

But over time, it has become clear that one problem associated with representative democracy is that only the interests of organized groups are heard, and the neediest in society are frequently unable to organize. While organized advocacy groups for the aged may speak out on issues of Social Security or Medicare—issues that affect 28 million older persons—few organized groups speak in behalf of the 1.4 million *poor* elderly who are recipients of the Supplemental Security Income program or the estimated 600,000 *homeless* elderly.[12]

Nonetheless, advocates for the elderly have become adept players within this multiplicity of interest groups, and have learned well how to organize to make their needs known in the political marketplace. They have learned the art of coalition building, and have successfully used not only the power of their own numbers, but the strength of nonelderly special-interest groups as well. Marmor[13] describes how coalition building between labor, advocacy groups for the elderly, farmers, nurses, and social workers was instrumental in pushing Congress to enact the Medicare program in 1965. While study groups for many years had been pointing out the vulnerability of older persons to catastrophic medical expenses, this rational argument of need was insufficient to overcome the strenuous professional objections of the American Medical Association. It was only when the weaker advocacy groups for the elderly joined forces with the powerful AFL-CIO that the rights of this minority were protected from the pressures of the interested combinations of the majority. And it is only through such coalition-building across age boundaries that an expanded long-term care program has any chance of adoption.

PREROGATIVES OF THE STATE

Another important theme in American political life is the protection of states' rights—those allowed to the individual states by the Constitution. As noted above, the framers of the Constitution wanted a limited central government and strong, autonomous states. The authority to be held by the central government is detailed in Article I, Section 8 of the Constitution and includes the following: the right to borrow money and collect taxes, to regulate commerce, coin money, establish a uniform naturalization rule, establish a post office, protect inventors and authors through patents and copyrights, set up lower courts, and raise and maintain armies and navies.

On the other hand, the Constitution specifically *prohibits* the states from engaging in certain activities, among them entering into treaties, laying duties on imports and exports, keeping troops, or entering into a state of war with foreign powers.

But, as can be seen, the Constitution is silent on the matter of which level of government should take responsibility for the financing and administering of social programs. While ambiguous, the Tenth Amendment to the Constitution seems to place such authority at the state level by allowing that "the powers not delegated to the United States by the Constitution, nor prohibited by it to the states, are reserved to the states respectively, or to the people." It is this phrase that explains both why we have few truly national social programs in the United States and why there is such variety from state to state in the federally funded programs that we do have. A historical look at welfare programs for the aged will illustrate the importance of this constitutional amendment.

Before 1975, cash assistance to poor older persons was provided through a federal/state grant mechanism. Under the Old Age Assistance program, the federal government gave each state money to provide these welfare payments. But the federal government also stipulated that in order to receive these federal dollars, the state had to match them with state revenues.

The federal government cannot force a state to participate in such a grant program. It cannot because to do so would mean that the federal government was dictating to the state how it should spend its own money—a constitutional violation. This leaves federal policymakers with one option if they really want the state to participate in achieving some nationally desirable policy goal. And that option is to entice states into participation by allowing them wide discretionary latitude regarding program administration. Thus, if it accepts money, a state can decide whom to serve, how to determine eligibility, and how generous and restrictive benefits and rules will be. Federal officials permit the existence of wide interstate variability within programs so that states will agree to offer them at all.

Medicaid is a federal/state grant program that provides an example of these federal limits as regards state autonomy. Until very recently, the officials of the state of Arizona refused to participate in the Medicaid program. They deemed that maintaining their county-supported health system for the poor was preferable to agreeing to federal program guidelines, even if it meant turning away federal grant dollars.

The only way in which interstate variability can be eliminated (or at least substantially reduced) is if the federal government assumes all costs of the program. In 1975, the Old Age Assistance program changed from a federal/state matching grant program to a national welfare program for the aged—the Supplemental Security Income (SSI) program. When the federal government assumed both fiscal and administrative responsibility, it was then able to insist on uniform rules of eligibility, uniform benefit payments, and standardized administrative practices. Until and unless federal officials agree to fully fund a national health or long-term care program, interstate variability will remain.

And it should be emphasized that federal officials have a compelling incentive to continue to share the cost of such large-scale programs with the states. Thus, a political trade-off will remain as we consider an expansion of our social and health programs, a trade-off between even larger *federal* financial obligations and a sharing of the burden with other levels of government, a situation which inevitably will continue to allow interstate program variability.

THE INDIVIDUAL AND THE STATE

One of the vignettes presented at the beginning of this chapter is of an elderly homeless couple who refuse all services although they are clearly in need. This vignette, sad and true, illustrates the limits of state intervention.

The state's right to step in to protect individuals when they appear to be endangering themselves has passed through many stages. The Progressive tradition that took hold in the United States during the first two decades of the twentieth century and persisted right through the middle of the 1960s gave a remarkable primacy to the idea of the state as parent, *parens patriae*.[14] During this time, reformers were much more attentive to the "needs" of disadvantaged groups than to their "rights." Routinely, Progressives tried to expand the discretionary powers of state officials and to endow the state with all the necessary authority to fulfill its goals.

Welfare applicants were required to demonstrate their worthiness by adhering to moral standards that were higher than the societal norm. Juvenile offenders were remanded to a juvenile court system in which all rules of evidence, assistance from counsel, and protection against self-incrimination were abandoned. Mentally retarded persons were sterilized and forbidden by law to marry. The paternalism that characterized state activity during these several decades often blinded reformers to the realities of what occurred in the day-to-day administration of the programs.

Not until the clients of service institutions rebelled in the 1960s did anyone begin to look with skepticism upon these good works. The vast discretionary power that came to be vested in an army of civil servants quietly and silently had begun trespassing upon the private lives and rights of millions of citizens.[15]

As a result of these abuses, public policies in recent decades have been designed more deliberately to reflect the kind of suspicion of government intervention that characterized America at an earlier time. More than a century before the Progressives took hold, the Bill of Rights reflected "less innocence about and more fear of government power."[16] The Bill of Rights was devised to protect the rights of individuals against the excesses of well-intentioned, democratically elected political rulers, excesses it was assumed would occur.

Today, our concern for the protection of civil rights mirrors that earlier time rather than our more recent Progressive history. Deinstitutionalization, treatment in the least restrictive environment, and community-based care each indicate an underlying urge to replace the sovereignty of the state with the sovereignty of the individual. "Over himself," wrote John Stuart Mill, "over his own body and mind, the individual is sovereign." While many health and social service professionals may feel that the pendulum has swung too far away from the Progressive ideal of the state as parent, policies today will only be feasible if they respect this deeply rooted American belief in the individual as sovereign and free.

In sum, then, it is our institutionalized political structures that help explain why our policies are so often fragmented and lacking in coherence, and why the outcomes of policy so often depart from their original ideals. The four themes that shape our political philosophy—separation of powers, democratic pluralism, states' rights, and the individual's rights—frame the environment of our policies and programs. In broad terms, they define what is feasible and serve as rationales to eliminate what is not. No advocate or program planner can meet success by ignoring them or dismissing their relevance.

Of equal importance in the policy environment is America's economic context. Much like our political philosophy, the economic principles we embrace as a country define and limit our range of social programs.

What Is an Economic System?

Although political and economic systems are related in important ways, they should not be confused with one another. The United States, for example, has blended the two in a capitalist democracy. Capitalism refers to a market economy in which resources are owned primarily by private individuals and groups. In a market economy, decisions as to which goods and services will be produced, how they will be produced, and who will use them are guided primarily by the interplay of buyers and sellers in the marketplace. These capitalist economic features are joined with a political system based on individual freedoms. Market economies can be democratic, as in the United States or somewhat more authoritarian, as in Spain.

The same is true of socialist economies. Socialism refers to an economy that depends heavily on the government to plan and make economic decisions and to own and control important economic resources. In the case of Sweden, democratic political processes guide a socialist-oriented economy; in the Soviet Union, a socialist economy is ruled by a single political party, the Communist Party.

Two hundred years ago, our government exercised little control in business matters, and individuals made almost all economic decisions. Today, things are more complicated. In place of a "laissez-faire" economy, we have a much more "mixed" economy in which three groups—consumers, producers, and governments—play major decisionmaking roles. Consumers continue to look for the best value for their money, producers seek the best returns for what they offer, and governments seek to promote the safety and welfare of the public and to provide services in the public interest. One of the biggest debates in our national life in recent decades has been over the extent to which government should be involved in our economic life.

The Government and the Economy

Since the Constitution was written, our country has grown enormously, and so has our government's role and responsibility. There are five major areas in which government units, federal, state and local, are involved with the economy. A list would include such governmental functions as (1) protection of the rights and freedoms of individuals—economic, political, religious—through our courts and the administration of our laws; (2) provision of goods and services in the interest of us all, such as highways, national defense, and education; (3) regulation that promotes fair economic competition and protects public health and safety; (4) promotion of economic growth and stabilization through various economic policies and programs dealing with interest rates, trade agreements, the money supply, and the like; and (5) direct support of individuals through programs to reduce hardships of those who cannot meet their minimum needs because of lack of employment or other specific circumstances.

These governmental functions cost money, and to carry them out in 1987, federal, state, and local governments spent about $1.6 trillion, or about $18,110 per household (based on approximately 88.5 million households in the United States). (Table 4-2.)

And all must be paid for with money raised in two basic ways—by taxing individuals and business and by borrowing. (In some cases we pay more directly for the public services we get.

Table 4-2. Expenditures of All Levels of Government, 1987

Expenditures	Billions of Dollars	Dollars per Household
Buying goods and services—national defense, education, highways, public safety	947	10,700
Direct assistance to individuals—Social Security, welfare, food stamps, unemployment, medical care	544	6,100
Interest on public debt	110	1,300
Miscellaneous	19	10
Total	1,620	18,110

SOURCE: *Economic Report of the President, 1989,* Table B-80. Washington, D.C.: U.S. Government Printing Office, p. 402.

Bridge tolls, postage stamps, tuition charges in public universities, deductibles and co-insurance charges in Medicare are examples of "user charges," and monies raised in these ways help pay for some of the costs of these services.) A display of the kinds of taxes collected by governments in 1987 is shown in Table 4-3.

As is obvious in these two tables, spending by all governments is greater than taxes generated. In 1987, this imbalance resulted in a $100 billion deficit, a deficit that can be financed only by borrowing.

Preoccupation with this deficit is keen among social program planners and advocates because unless expenditures and revenues come more into balance no new program initiatives are likely to be proposed. Even a no-growth position will lead to increased deficits through the impact of inflation. (Providing the *same* services this year as last will simply cost more.)

Remedying the deficit situation presents elected officials with one of two equally unpalatable political choices. They can propose a spending reduction, that is, program cutbacks, or they can propose revenue enhancement, that is, higher taxes. To date, politicians have been unwilling to make either of these hard short-term political decisions. Hence, the deficit grows.

Of course, there is a third scenario that in the 1980 presidential campaign was commonly referred to as "voodoo economics." In this scenario, it is possible to expand programs, reduce taxes, and dissolve the deficit. Its major assumption is that a strong performance by the economy—that is, strong economic growth—will automatically generate enough new revenues to accomplish all three

Table 4-3. Revenues of All Levels of Government, 1987

Revenue Sources	Billions of Dollars	Percent of Total
Personal income	591	39
Corporate profit taxes	136	9
Indirect business taxes, including sales and property	374	25
Payroll taxes, i.e., social security, unemployment	408	27
Total	1,509	100

SOURCE: *Economic Report of the President, 1989*, Table B-80. Washington, D.C.: U.S. Government Printing Office, p. 402.

goals. Unfortunately, a large deficit precludes a robust economy, since the money used to meet the debt service becomes unavailable for more productive enterprises.

Most economic analysts today are skeptical of this third scenario and agree that the only cure for our current deficit ills can be found in one of the two more painful prescriptions noted above, that is, cutting program expenditures or raising taxes.

Capitalism and Its Implications

The acceptance by American society of market theory and capitalism as the basis of its economic system has a number of implications for our social programs. Three are especially prominent—an acceptance of income inequality; a view that government intervenes in the private market only when there is market failure; and a belief that self-interest and competition are the fuels of productivity.

WINNERS AND LOSERS

The anatomy of the American economy contrasts sharply with the egalitarian structure of its polity.[17] While our political rights and freedoms honor the equality of each man and woman under the law, the reward structure of a market economy generates substantial inequality regarding income and wealth. In our economic system, goods and services are not distributed through government, but are made available for purchase through the private market. An individual remains self-sufficient and a consumer in our market by generating income as a producer.

Most of us "work for a living." That means that we sell our skills in the marketplace in return for a salary or wage. And the level of income that each of us can command in the open market determines our relative well-being in society. What determines our income? Four elements are usually seen as determining the productive contribution each of us makes to the economy.

The first is our acquired skills. What I have to sell in the marketplace reflects my entire life history. My health history, my educational attainment, my previous job experiences, my family background—each of these can add to or detract from my marketability. A youngster from a poor family, who may have suffered early from nutritional deficiencies, who performed poorly in school, and who dropped out before graduation will have a lower chance of success in the marketplace than a youngster from a middle-class family. A young woman of 23 who has attained an M.B.A. from Harvard will command a higher salary in the marketplace than a 23-year-old who has only completed secretarial school. Thus, acquired skills will be a factor in the personal equation of one's market success.

Natural or innate abilities are a second determinant of market income. Some individuals are smarter than others, some more verbally facile. One person may have a mathematical aptitude that translates into a career in space engineering, while another excels in eye-hand coordination and becomes a star receiver for the Chicago Bears. There is even evidence to suggest that height may provide an advantage in the marketplace. A comparison of presidential candidates has shown the taller to be more likely to be elected than the shorter in a statistically significant number of cases! Natural talents and endowments influence our incomes across a lifetime.

A third element that explains uneven income distribution across the population is personal effort. Differences in incomes that are associated with differences in effort generally are regarded by the public as fair. If I put in an eight-hour day and my office mate half that amount, I would expect our salaries to be different. If I work overtime, or if I work two jobs, compensation should be commensurate with this effort. Such arrangements not only are fair to the individual involved, but in the broader perspective contribute to the social good. Incentives to greater effort, that is, more compensation, encourage greater market productivity. And greater productive output in the economy translates into a higher standard of living for everyone.

Finally, the supply-and-demand features of the economy shape the differential incomes found in the population. Currently, for example, we are experiencing a shortage of registered nurses. As the supply declines, and the demand for nursing services remains steady or increases, wages will rise and the income of nurses will go up. Sometimes it is individual occupations that experience changes in supply or demand (e.g., we have a shortage of engineers but a glut of physicians), sometimes it is changes in the overall economy (e.g., high interest rates reduce building starts, which leads to slowdowns and layoffs in the lumber industry).

These four elements—acquired skills, natural abilities, effort, and supply and demand—each have a hand in determining what our personal income and the distribution of income in our society will be. And they explain why poverty and inequality of income persist. Individuals do not start out with equal capacities to compete for income in the marketplace. Those disadvantaged through their natural and/or acquired abilities often have few marketable skills and little ability to earn a minimally adequate income.

It is for those among us who are "economically disadvantaged" that the government steps in with income supplementation (e.g., food stamps and welfare) and with remedial services (e.g., basic literacy courses and job training programs). For older persons, who typically retire from the marketplace, government provisions take the form of Social Security and Medicare benefits, as well as Supplemental Security Income and other social services.

Since such government redistribution alters the market-generated distribution of income, it is always suspect. While the public generally applauds redistributive measures for their equalizing function, it often believes that such measures reduce individual incentives for greater productive efforts. This concern usually does not extend to older persons who are no longer expected to participate in the market, however.

THE "FREE" MARKET

We all have heard references to the importance of a "free market." From what should the market be free? Government intervention. Two arguments are brought forward as to why government should stay out of market operations as much as possible. One is based on efficiency, the other on individual liberty.

Under circumstances of a perfect market, the voluntary exchanges between buyers and sellers that characterize the system result in just the right things being produced, in just the right quantity, and at just the right price (that is, at a price that people will be willing to pay). A competitive market transmits signals to producers that reflect the values of consumers. The producer has the incentive to make what consumers want in the least costly way.

Nobody is asked to evaluate what is good for the system or for the society; if the individual merely pursues his or her own economic self-interest, he or she will automatically serve the social welfare. Thus, the market is efficient if it is left to freely reflect the preferences of consumers and producers without government interference.

Yet this market operations ideal often is not found in reality. Several kinds of market failure require government intervention. Let us review the major ones.

First, the ideal market scenario presumes a competition among providers that will lead each to strive to produce more and more efficiently, thus lowering prices as time goes on. But the image of a myriad of small producers, each competing on an equal footing, suffers from the same limitations described earlier in our discussion of interest-group politics. A number of small interest groups can be overwhelmed by one large one. Whether it is the interests of a welfare rights organization overwhelmed by the interests of the AFL-CIO, or the interests of a small independent auto maker overwhelmed by the interests of General Motors, certain interests have a competitive advantage. This is especially true if the firm has a monopoly position. So government often steps in to protect smaller firms from being placed at a competitive disadvantage by a firm that threatens to hold a monopoly in the market.

A second way in which the ideal market situation may fail is when producers do not take into account externalities associated with their operation. A producer's most efficient means of production (the means that will lead to the lowest price for the consumer) for example, may involve social costs not borne by the producer. The clearest cases of such "externalities" are found in industries that pollute our air, water, or soil. A polluting chemical plant, for example, is not directly hurt in the marketplace by its practices. On the contrary, were the plant officials to install pollution control devices when their competitors did not, they would have to raise prices and hence be at a competitive price disadvantage in the market! Pollution affects others in society and should not be allowed. So, in such a case, societal protection is the higher good that supports governmental intervention, intervention that forces the producer to attend to the pollution even if this means tampering with free market operations.

Finally, as noted earlier, a free market does leave at a disadvantage those who are unequipped to participate as producers, and consequently, as consumers. Government steps in here in our society to alter the market distribution of income and protect the disadvantaged through public redistributive means.

So, while it might adversely affect the efficiency of market operations, we sometimes allow government interference for a higher social good. Nonetheless, government intervention in the economy is permitted reluctantly and sparingly in the United States, and only for a compelling reason.

Government is also encouraged to stay out of the market to preserve individual freedoms. Western economics is at heart an economics of the individual. Individuals organize voluntary economic associations (the firm), and individuals earn and allocate income.[18] Much as our political philosophy restrains government from encroaching on individual liberties, our economic system encourages freedom of the individual in the marketplace.

Perhaps the most well-known person who has linked the notion of political freedoms with economic freedoms is Milton Friedman. "Viewed as a means to the end of political freedom," Friedman notes, "economic arrangements are important because of their effect on the concentration or dispersion of power. The kind of economic organization that provides economic freedom directly, namely, competitive capitalism, also promotes political freedom because it separates economic power from political power and in this way enables one to offset the other."[19] In Friedman's view, the role of government should be limited to providing a forum for determining the "rules of the game" and in acting as an umpire to interpret and enforce the rules decided upon.

Friedman's outspoken opinions opposing redistributive social welfare measures are well documented. For example, he would abolish our Social Security system. He believes that mandatory Social Security infringes on individual freedoms by depriving individuals of control of a sizable fraction of their incomes and by forcing them to devote it to a particular purpose, without choice. He believes that the existence of Social Security has negatively affected the market in that it has "inhibited competition in the sale of annuities and the development of retirement arrangements."[20] Friedman's preference would be to let individuals purchase annuities for themselves, and to make as a public charge the man who does not provide for his old age.

While considered radical in his view toward government intervention in the market, Friedman nonetheless does illustrate the close connection that is held in the minds of Americans between political and economic freedoms. Our choice of a competitive market system, one that emphasizes individual effort, is very compatible with our choice of a political system in which individual rights are glorified and the competition of special interests is thought to lead to the greatest good for all.

Our economic system, like our political system, greatly influences the shape of our social welfare policies. Our acceptance of market theory and capitalism leads to a tolerance by our society of the unequal distribution of income and wealth. Thus, the poor we shall always have with us. Strategies to address problems facing the poor are likely to continue to emphasize integration in the market system (for example, job training), rather than compensation for obvious market weaknesses (for example, a guaranteed minimum income).

Our view that the role of government should be limited, that is, that government should intervene *only* when the market fails, leads to government that is reactive rather than proactive. It also allows only weak protections for those who may be exploited by unscrupulous market practices.

And finally, acceptance of market capitalism supports the belief that people should earn their rewards, that they need incentives in order to work hard, and that pragmatism and efficiency are of high priority. This set of values, with those discussed earlier, both limits what is possible by government and limits what is acceptable in terms of government intervention. There is a marked preference in our society to seek private sector solutions to social problems before developing public sector solutions. And, there is a deep suspicion of any measures that are overtly redistributive, that is, that directly seek to alter the natural income distribution that results from the free operation of a competitive market.

What It All Means

Why is it important for service providers and advocates for the elderly to have a clear understanding of America's political and economic culture? And what implications do these systems have for an elderly population that is increasingly diverse?

The answer to the first question is perhaps the most obvious. Those wishing to promote new policies or alter existing ones only will be successful if they understand the structural constraints and opportunities presented by our political and economic systems. If one were to review the many recommendations that flow from our White House Conferences on Aging, one could identify immediately those recommendations that have a chance of implementation and those that do not. What distinguishes the former is their sensitivity to the matters discussed in this chapter.

Too often a lack of action on the part of politicians and others is attributed to the constraints of our resources. But more likely, our loftier reform goals are thwarted because they are incompatible with certain deeply held national beliefs. Let us examine one example.

Does a call for a comprehensive national health insurance plan fail merely because its costs are deemed too high? No, not for that reason alone. It also fails because it seems to threaten our individual freedoms—Will I still be able to choose my own doctor under such a system, or will the government assign one to me? It fails because it presents a specter of a massive federal bureaucracy and an army of intrusive civil servants. It fails because such a system threatens to fix and limit prices that physicians can charge. Shouldn't physicians be rewarded for the money, time, and effort that they have put into their training by earning generous incomes? A suspicion exists that a national health insurance scheme is somehow incompatible with what we cherish within our political and economic systems. We fear the intrusiveness and inefficiencies such a system might bring, and we are as yet unwilling to risk its unknown outcomes. We prefer to cling to the system that we already know. Analysis such as this will alert the advocate to watch out for reform proposals that conflict with certain features of our political and economic system, and therefore are unlikely to be adopted.

Perhaps the strongest lesson to be learned from an examination of the functioning of our political system is that policies are blunt instruments. Because policies are rooted in legislation, they reflect a consensus among parties who may define a particular problem differently and who may prefer quite different solutions. The outcome of politics is often a program that no one prefers but one to which the fewest number of persons object. This kind of program usually leads only to incremental changes, not radical reform. Advocates, then must be prepared to accept the limited programs that our system, with its diffusion of power and emphasis on consensus, is likely to develop.

The role of states in programs also will remain strong. Our acceptance of state sovereignty presents a barrier to the nationalizing of many programs. While it is true that since the 1930s there has been some shift in program responsibility from the states to the federal government, each step in such a shift has been a painful one. Federalism still implies a sharing of program responsibility, and fiscal federalism still implies a cost-sharing responsibility. The so-called Reagan Revolution reasserted the importance of the states in the development and financing of social programs, and this shift in policy is not likely to be reversed in the near term.

Our preference for not tampering with the operations of the marketplace continues to cause us to seek either private-sector solutions to social problems or solutions that are patterned after private-sector initiatives. Part of the reason for the political success of Social Security is that it seems like a private insurance plan. One pays premiums and then can claim benefits on retirement. Terms such as "contribution" and "earned rights" have masked the compulsory, public nature of this program and have led to its popular acceptance. Such terms have also encouraged the illusion of a prudent citizen saving for his or her old age, an image consistent with our belief that an individual should be self-sufficient. We can expect that future public programs also will require a cloaking in the mantle of private-sector language.

Long-term care policies already appear to be taking such shape. Many of the legislative initiatives that were considered in the recently concluded 100th Congress would have paid for long-term care services through a payroll tax, just like those for Social Security and Medicare. In his bill, Senator Edward M. Kennedy (D, Mass.) would have expanded coverage of home- and community-based services as well as paid for the first six months of nursing home care. As noted when the bill was introduced, "This plan is a universal social insurance program modeled on the successful experience of Medicare and Social Security. All Americans will contribute, and all seniors, disabled children, and disabled adults eligible for Medicare will benefit."[21]

The bill submitted by Representative Claude Pepper (D, Fla.), H.R. 3436, would have expanded Medicare coverage to include long-term home care for chronically ill individuals by eliminating the cap on income that would be subject to the 1.45 percent Medicare payroll tax ($45,000 in 1988). This proposal was promoted as being "self-financing" and "budget neutral"; the two terms were aimed at allaying fears about the costs of such an expansion.

It is likely that future long-term care initiatives also will model themselves after social insurance, a model consistent with our belief that government benefits are more comfortably considered insurance than what they really are, benefits from the government.

Accompanying these public proposals is a parallel development. Encouraged by public-sector support, private long-term care insurance plans are expanding. In 1985, the Congress set up a task force that was to submit recommendations concerning the promotion of private long-term care insurance and to suggest ways to generate consumer confidence in such plans.

Reporting out in the autumn of 1987, the task force concluded that while private long-term care insurance cannot provide a total solution for the financing of long-term care for everyone, "large segments of society can and should provide for their own future needs."[22] In addition, the task force adopted several recommendations that dealt with creating awareness of the need for long-term care insurance and stimulating a demand for more of it, as well as recommendations that would protect consumers against possible market abuses. Already, Congress has introduced countless bills that would encourage employers to offer and individuals to purchase such insurance through the granting of income tax relief. And in the summer of 1988, Senator David Durenburger (R, Minn.), introduced a bill that would "establish a program of voluntary certification of long-term care insurance policies."[23]

These developments illustrate that as we seek new solutions to compelling social problems, we first explore solutions that are compatible with our private market preferences. It is clear that only those policy options that are consistent with our country's political philosophy and economic principles will engender serious consideration.

RESPONDING TO DIVERSITY

Diversity within American society is not new. The Statue of Liberty, a gift from another nation, is testimony to America's reputation as a country ready to welcome the tired, hungry, and poor huddled masses of other nations. Once on our shores, these immigrants were expected to integrate into mainstream society and become full partners in the country's political and economic life. And for the most part, that scenario has been played out by generations of immigrants.

Religious diversity also has been accepted since this country's founding. The Constitution guarantees individuals the free exercise of religion and forbids the adoption of a single state religion. As a result, Christians, Jews, Moslems, and others coexist without the sectarian strife so often characteristic of other nations.

Economic mainstreaming also was expected of new immigrants to this country. Until recently, a lack of education or limited language skills did not exclude an individual from finding some place in the market. Today, however, even the most menial jobs often require a high school diploma, and most jobs require basic English literacy skills. Thus the opportunity for economic mainstreaming has diminished somewhat for those with few acquired skills or innate abilities.

Whether this country's assimilative approach will work with a diverse aged population remains to be seen. As Taeuber notes in Chapter 1, a very large, diverse elderly population is a novel experience. How readily can our political structure respond to demands that are diverse and diffuse? How readily will our politicians be able to distinguish among the various needs of this heterogeneous group? Will our economic system be able to channel the breadth of human capital that will exist among this group? These are questions that will need to be answered in the 1990s and beyond.

Notes

1. Okun, A.M. *Equality and Efficiency: The Big Tradeoff*. Washington, D.C.: Brookings Institution, 1975, p. vii.

2. De Tocqueville, A. In R.D. Heffner (Ed.) *Democracy in America*. New York: Mentor Books, 1956, p. 194.

3. Bellah, R.N., R. Madsen, W.M. Sullivan, A. Swidler, and S.M. Tipton. *Habits of the Heart: Individualism and Commitment in American Life*. Berkeley, Calif.: University of California Press, 1985.

4. Wilensky, H.L. and C.N. Lebeaux. *Industrial Society and Social Welfare*. New York: The Free Press, 1965.

5. Feller, B. National Center for Health Statistics. "Americans Needing Help to Function at Home." No. 92, DHHS Pub. No. (PHS) 83-1250, Public Health Service, Hyattsville, Md., September 1983.

6. Stone, R. National Center for Health Statistics. "Aging in the Eighties: Age 65 Years and Over—Use of Community Services," No. 124, DHHS Pub. No. (PHS) 86-1250, Public Health Service, Hyattsville, Md., September 1986.

7. Lazenby, H., K. Levit, and D. Waldo. "National Health Expenditures, 1985," No. 6, HCFA Pub. No. 03232, September 1986, p. 8.

8. Derthick, M. *Policymaking for Social Security.* Washington, D.C.: The Brookings Institution, 1979, p. 207.

9. Lazenby, "National Health Expenditures," p. 22.

10. *Budget of the United States Government, Fiscal Year 1990*. Washington, D.C.: Government Printing Office, 1989, pp. 5–115.

11. Hamilton, A., J. Madison, and J. Jay. *The Federalist Papers*. New York: Mentor Books, 1961, p. 324.

12. *Social Security Bulletin* 52, 6 (June 1989): 17.

13. Marmor, T.R. *The Politics of Medicare*. Chicago: Aldine Publishing Co., 1973.

14. Rothman, D.J. "The state as parent: Social policy in the progressive era." In W. Gaylin, I. Glasser, S. Marcus, and D. Rothman (Eds.) *Doing Good: The Limits of Benevolence*. New York: Pantheon Books, 1978, p. 69.

15. Glasser, I. "Prisoners of benevolence: Power versus liberty in the welfare state." In W. Gaylin, I. Glasser, S. Marcus, and D. Rothman (Eds.) *Doing Good: The Limits of Benevolence*. New York: Pantheon Books, 1978, pp. 107–108.

16. Ibid., p. 99.

17. Okun, *Equality and Efficiency*. p. 32.

18. Thurow, L.C. *The Zero-Sum Society*. New York: Basic Books, 1980, p. 178.

19. Friedman, M. *Capitalism and Freedom*. Chicago: University of Chicago Press, 1962, p. 9.

20. Ibid., p. 189.

21. *Congressional Record*. August 3, 1988, S10770.

22. Task Force on Long-Term Care Financing. *Report to Congress*. Washington, D.C.: U.S. Government Printing Office, 1988, p. 11.

23. *Congressional Record*. July 13, 1988, S9592.

CHAPTER FIVE

The Politics of Entitlement and the Politics of Productivity

HARRY R. MOODY

There is a strange silence in American political discourse about old age. It is a silence about the productivity and social contribution of older people. In some respects that public silence is puzzling because gerontologists in recent years have been eloquent on the theme of productive aging.[1,2] Some discussions among leaders in the field have approached the question of the aging of America in terms that put the productivity of older people squarely at the center of their agenda.[3–5] But in broader political terms, there has been only silence. This article examines what is known as the politics of productivity and addresses the question of whether the silence of the past can be replaced by a fruitful dialogue in the future.

We may start by acknowledging that, historically, political liberals have been characteristically troubled by the politics of productivity, or, the politics of jobs. The rhetoric of productivity and appeals to the need for economic growth have been dominated by free-market conservatives. Conservatives have set the terms of debate. The result is that any open concern about productivity, such as worry about capital formation, seems to suggest a covert way to cut government spending in favor of the private sector. But less government assistance is by no means the only policy position that might follow from greater concern about productivity.

In some respects, we should acknowledge at the outset that entitlement and productivity are indeed opposing ideas. Entitlement programs such as Social Security and Medicare constitute a transfer of consuming power to the aged as a categorical group. Other benefit programs, such as public education or subsidies for farmers, are distributed to categorical groups without any question about their productivity. Accordingly, by this definition, those programs also constitute "entitlements." Asking what older people should contribute seems opposed to asking what they should receive. But it is a false and dangerous polarization to imagine that we must somehow choose, once and for all, between entitlement and productivity.[6] A sound and balanced policy framework will demand elements of both. Yet acknowledging the need for an aging population to be socially productive is a political step that liberals and advocates of the elderly have found hard to take.

There are reasons for this liberal reluctance. If productivity and entitlement are opposites, then why give ground to opponents of the welfare state? Why risk giving up the hard-won benefits? The reluctance here is partly rhetorical, but it is also a matter of political tactics. It is argued that, just as liberals resist workfare programs for welfare recipients, so should they resist demands that the elderly be "productive." But today the time may be ripe for a tactical shift in this debate. Analysts of political trends since the 1960s have noted that liberal political defeats on the so-called social issues (family, patriotism, crime) have repeatedly come from allowing conservatives to capture the high ground of the debate.[7] The rhetoric of productivity has also been captured, and even monopolized, by the right wing.

Unless liberals recapture the middle ground that *unites* the politics of productivity and the politics of entitlement, there is a danger of divisiveness from debates about distribution of benefits and entitlements. In an era of budget deficits and fiscal constraint, that danger is already acute. In part, recent debates about generational equity[8, 9] reflect exactly this divisiveness arising from a "zero-sum" game that has, for too long, excluded considerations of productivity.[10] Any further gains in the policies of aging or broad-based policy initiatives will probably require an expanding economy. The politics of productivity assumes that the elderly can contribute to that economic expansion, and in that way re-legitimize their importance and usefulness. There lies the challenge of the future.

A compelling reason for taking up this challenge is found in the theme of this book: the diversity of the aging population. "Diversity" as a catchword has also been something of a cliché among gerontologists. As an empirical matter, it is undoubtedly true that the population aged 65 years and older has become more diverse in recent years. That empirical trend is hardly a matter of debate. What is more important is how diversity operates in today's political environment.

Gerontologists like to stress that the aged are not a homogeneous group. They are right to do so, and not only for scientific reasons. Stressing diversity is rhetorically useful as a means of refuting those who are allegedly promoting a "new stereotype" of a uniformly well-to-do elderly population.[11] Advocates of the aged stress diversity in order to remind us that the elderly poor are still with us. And the next line in this conventional liberal argument is usually to plead for a minimum benefit or liberalization of means-tested programs. For how else can we be sure of reaching the "truly needy" under universal social entitlements?

But diversity is a two-edged sword. There is risk in this strategy and, more generally, in the rhetoric of diversity. As we have learned in recent years, talk about diversity in the context of redistributive policy also gives an opening for policies that shift entitlement programs toward an ability-to-pay criterion: for example, the 1983 Social Security amendments taxing benefits for upper-income beneficiaries or the 1988 Medicare Catastrophic Coverage Act financed by a progressive income surtax. Advocates for the elders were characteristically uncomfortable with both moves.

But stressing diversity without challenging the overall framework of redistributive politics is an invitation to incremental change in entitlement programs. Recent policy changes did not institute a means test, but they did constitute an erosion of the universality of benefits in favor of equity claims: from each according to ability to pay. The problem, as usual, is that under this incrementalism, the framework of redistribution was simply taken for granted. A more imaginative response would be to challenge directly the hegemony, or predominance, of the politics of redistribution and consider an alternative politics of productivity. That, in essence, is the strategy urged in this chapter.

Recent Politics of Aging in America

The prospects for a productivity strategy can best be appraised by reviewing some recent political history that bears on aging policy. In the decade of the 1980s productivity became a potent political theme, and Republicans in the Reagan era quickly seized the high ground of productivity rhetoric. Like John F. Kennedy in 1960, Ronald Reagan in 1980 promised to "get America moving" and to lead us to a brighter future.

This attitude by politicians toward productivity has been vindicated, to the consternation of liberals, by economic events since 1982. Reagan-era economic policies produced tangible economic gains for a majority of the population: low inflation, declining unemployment, and the longest period of economic growth since World War II. While presiding over economic successes, Republicans legitimated their version of "productivity." Their success left liberals with only two political strategies: worrying about subgroups of the population who were worse off than before or protesting that things were sure to get worse for everyone in the future. But liberals in the 1988 election did not succeed in making their case on this issue to the American public.

The Republican claims, of course, did ignore several major unresolved problems: (1) an accumulating federal deficit that constrains new federal initiatives and still casts a shadow over future prosperity; (2) a long-term adverse change in U.S. economic competitiveness (for example, trade deficits); (3) serious inequalities and the persistence of poverty among subgroups of the population (those in the farm-belt and rust-belt industries, minorities, and single women). Each of these problems is real, and that is well appreciated by serious policy analysts.

Despite some misgivings, the public in 1988 expressed an ambivalent hope for the future and therefore voted for the status quo. But the policy environment in place by the end of the 1980s was by no means a victory for conservatives. During the Reagan era, conservatives did not succeed in persuading the public that less government is better. Nor did they succeed in dismantling the welfare state or in challenging the legitimacy of entitlement programs for the elderly. What they did succeed in doing, largely through the impact of tax cuts, a huge federal deficit, and the Gramm-Rudman Act, was to prevent consideration of any large or bold new programs for domestic spending. That legacy is perhaps the most important heritage of Reagan's social policy and is likely to be felt throughout the 1990s. It will shape the politics of aging no less than other fields of domestic activity.

How in fact has this broad legacy affected the policy of aging? Let us take the three big problems cited above—the deficit, international competition, and persistent poverty—and ask in each case how the policy of aging will cope with this significant legacy of the Reagan years.

As to the budget deficit, the most telling example of a new policy environment is apparent in the 1988 Medicare Catastrophic Coverage Act with its requirement that this new entitlement be both "revenue-neutral" (Gramm-Rudman) and "generationally neutral" (the new principle of generational equity). Against the limits set by the deficit, Congress decreed that new benefits would be financed by the elderly themselves. And in view of the diversity of the aging population, tax policies were devised on an ability-to-pay basis rather than in the manner of more uniform entitlements in social insurance. These developments mark a sharp break with the past.[12]

As to international competitiveness, aging entitlement programs are also under scrutiny if not yet serious political pressure. There is a growing feeling, right or wrong, that entitlement spending, particularly on the elderly, is a drag on U.S. economic growth. This view is linked to an image of the aging society as a "spectre of decline."[13] Furthermore, on an international level, there is recognition that the United States, along with Western Europe and Japan, is now facing an unprecedented demographic challenge of population aging.[14] That challenge brings with it interlocking questions about pension costs, capital formation, economic innovation, and financing of the welfare state in demographically mature societies.[15]

As to the persistence of poverty, there is a new realization, among the policy elite if not yet among the general public, that the aged population is not uniformly rich or poor but rather economically diverse. But again, what does "diversity" imply for policymakers? Apparently, it does not signify the need for initiatives to target new benefits for the elderly poor: for example, an expansion of access to Supplemental Security Income (SSI). On the contrary, the new recognition of economic diversity has turned attention not to the promotion of more equitable or generous benefits but to new kinds of burdens and taxes. It has led, for example, to redistributive tax policies directed at the more affluent elderly, on Social Security (1983) and Medicare (1988). But higher taxes for the more affluent elderly may do little to help the elderly poor. If no initiatives are undertaken to help the disadvantaged elderly, their plight is likely to remain in the future.[16]

In sum, the combination of a large federal deficit, international economic competition, and the increased heterogeneity of the elderly population itself has created a dramatically different policy environment from the one that existed in the 1960s and 1970s, a period when older people improved their condition remarkably. It is unlikely that earlier historical conditions will be repeated. Yet the debate among advocates for the elderly tends to be limited in its view of what can be done in the new environment today. Overall, we see mainly defensive responses: damage control, timid incremental reforms, rear-guard defense of vested interests, and adherence to the status quo. There is little serious debate about new policy alternatives.

We need to call attention here to an assumption about government policy that underlies virtually all discussion of the policy of aging. That assumption can be summed up in a single phrase: the elderly are entitled. The assumption is that older people are a needy and worthy population, deserving of public support. Once granted that assumption, the policy debate on the benefit side becomes a matter of deciding *which* subgroups among the elderly are most needy and how best to target benefits. On the revenue side, the debate becomes a matter of deciding which groups are going to pay for benefits for the aged—the general population, younger workers (for example, through Social Security taxes), older people themselves, the affluent elderly, even the dead (for example, through inheritance taxes).

In short, this entire policy debate revolves around the politics of redistribution, which is grounded on an assumption that the policy process exists to correlate "need" (however defined) with "resources" (wherever obtained). This policy framework also has a political correlate. It is evidently tied to the traditional liberal Democratic agenda—"tax and spend, elect and elect"—inaugurated by the New Deal but enshrined in welfare state policies from that time until the present.[17]

What is passed over in silence is the question of alternatives: Is there an alternative to this conventional policy debate with its hegemony of redistribution over productivity?

The Need for the Politics of Productivity

The essence of talk about productivity is that it shifts our discourse away from a zero-sum game. As Thurow[18] has emphasized, the need to restore American competitiveness means rethinking our assumptions about productivity and redistribution. Instead of debating how to cut a fixed pie (a zero-sum situation) or redistributing existing resources, we look at how to enlarge the pie or create new resources. In the field of aging, instead of talking exclusively about age-based entitlements, we begin talking about contributions by older people to society. Instead of seeing older people entirely as a needy population or as a burden on society, we begin to see older people as a resource in an interdependent society.

This shift in thinking is needed for the following reasons. First, there is the leitmotif of this book: diversity. Considering the aged as a productive resource better fits the emerging diversity of the aging population itself. Some older people are needy, others can have contributive roles and responsibilities. Some can continue to work at age 65, others for reasons of health need to retire much earlier, and still others will find productive contributions outside the monetized labor force. Acknowledging diversity need not mean abolishing or curbing entitlement programs, for instance, raising the eligibility age for retirement benefits. But it might mean redesigning the old-age welfare state to include programs that respond to the heterogeneity of the aged population. The choice is *not* simply between age or need as a basis for entitlement.

The second reason for a shift in thinking is a political reality: the need to gain political legitimacy for new domestic programs. Talking about "investing in human resources," as many liberals do today, is a way of reclaiming the rhetoric of productivity too long appropriated by free-market conservatives. The fact is that claims of need are politically unpersuasive in a period of government deficit and real-income stagnation. Hence, the economic metaphor of "investment" becomes attractive. Liberals thus try to legitimate more public spending on education, family care, welfare reform, and so on in terms of "investment in human resources." In the process, they hope to make those programs less vulnerable when conservatives attack them as give-aways or claims by special interests.

Third, there is the threat of divisiveness. Competition over a limited pie inevitably ends up pitting one group against another, whether we are talking about subgroups among the elderly or about the young versus the old. Pitting one group against another is not a recipe for long-range political success in a pluralistic society. But a politics of redistribution, particularly in times of fiscal constraint, runs precisely that risk. A compelling argument for the politics of productivity is that it represents our best alternative to a politics of "beggar thy neighbor" under entitlement spending for special interest groups. The politics of productivity moves the policy agenda in a more hopeful direction: toward investing in people today for productivity tomorrow, toward new alliances and coalitions among interest groups, toward values with a conservative flavor (for example, self-help), and ultimately toward a larger pie where one group's gains are not seen as another group's losses.

Fourth, the politics of productivity recasts the role of government in an aging society. Instead of government as an arbiter of competing interests or a channel for transfer payments, government becomes an enabling force for economic growth. Public policy for an aging population can become linked with initiatives to make America more productive: for example, the retraining of older workers or displaced homemakers in order to prevent old age poverty tomorrow.[19] A more affirmative government policy can well be justified in terms of both preventive action and individual self-reliance.

Finally, the politics of productivity reinforces a more positive role and image of old age itself. Advocates for the elderly have dwelt too long on the "failure model" of old age.[20] Instead of casting the elderly in the outdated stereotype of a vulnerable or needy group in order to justify entitlement programs, the politics of productivity allows us to recognize gains in the education or economic well-being of older people and then to use those gains as a basis for new contributive roles, rather than allowing those gains to become a pretext for cutting age-based entitlements.

Alternatives to the Status Quo

The most vexing question about this call for a politics of productivity is simply: Is it politically feasible? Can the politics of productivity work? Does it have a serious future? Even if one agrees with the argument offered here or is attracted by a productivity strategy for aging, those who are skeptical may be inclined to say that this new policy agenda is simply utopian or politically impossible.

The problem here can be summed up by the contrast between the discourse that appears in the policy literature on aging and the discourse that appears in public debate on the policy of aging in America. Some policy analysts and gerontologists recognize the need for a productivity strategy. But the discourse about aging in the political world is couched exclusively in terms of needs and rights, not in terms of productivity or the common good. As the election of 1988 demonstrated, politicians get elected by promising not to touch age-based entitlements such as Social Security or Medicare. Whatever policy analysts may think about generational equity or productivity strategies, their discourse has had no effect on public opinion or on political discourse. To put it bluntly: The two domains, policy analysis and political rhetoric, seem to exist in different worlds. They are moving further and further apart.

Let us take as an example the recent work by Aaron, Bosworth, and Burtless with the provocative title *Can America Afford to Grow Old?*[21] The book itself is not a summary of recent arguments about generational equity. But it does respond to many of the worries engendered by that debate. Nor is the book, despite its title, another gloomy forecast in the style of the "spectre of decline" literature so familiar in recent years. The book's major conclusion is that over the next seventy-five years America faces significant distributional choices in how to pay for the costs of an aging society.[22] The analysis offered in this book helps convert some of the apocalyptic scenarios conjured up by the generational equity debate into real-world choices facing policymakers: choices about payroll taxes, the magnitude of the Social Security surplus, the impact of retirement incentives on successive cohorts of elderly, and so on.

But in constructing simulations of economic behavior, the authors focus heavily on macroeconomic dimensions of pension policy or the distributional consequences of policy options. There is far less treatment of labor market participation by older people or attention to issues of human capital formation and worker productivity envisaged in terms of life span. And there lies the problem. We should not accept simulations or scenarios that take for granted the continued hegemony of redistributive politics. The chief argument of this chapter is that the labor market and the broader productivity of older Americans are crucial if we are to break out of the policy gridlock imposed by the politics of entitlement.

We can put the matter starkly by the following contrast, which requires no sophisticated economic simulation. What would happen if, instead of a drop in labor market participation by older male workers since 1950, the level of participation had risen in correlation with gains in life expectancy? For instance, what would happen if, instead of an average retirement age of 61 today, we had an average retirement age of 68? Given improvement in health status and longevity, a higher age of retirement is certainly feasible right now rather than waiting for it to begin in 2010, as envisaged under the Social Security reforms of 1983.

Then, consider another alternative. What would happen if, instead of an effective retirement age now hovering in the low sixties, we had widespread retirement at 55, on the model of the military, some sectors of civil service, or Third World countries where early compulsory retirement is a common response to high unemployment rates among educated workers? The exact economic impact of these two contrasting scenarios would be useful to simulate. But even a casual analysis suggests that decreasing or raising average retirement age could have an enormous impact on aggregate output in the economy: a difference of 13 years between the two extreme scenarios, or a difference of more than 25 percent of total worklife (optimistically, forty years).

The point in contrasting these two scenarios is to remind us that retirement as an entitlement is a social choice, and therefore a distributional choice. The distributional choice implicit here should never be masked by simulations of pension policy that take for granted a retirement age that remains remarkably low in light of impressive increases in life expectancy (from age 60), dramatically rising levels of education, improved health status of the young old: in short, these and other factors that would seemingly characterize the older population as a potent factor in any equation of national productivity. Alternatives are theoretically possible. But the fact remains that social norms and individual preference, along with incentives provided by business and government, have converged to keep the average age of retirement falling in the United States as in most other advanced industrialized countries.

Viewed in historical terms, retirement itself, as a social institution, is something of an anomaly. Its history as an institutionalized practice is very, very recent.[23] There is no reason to regard it as historically inevitable. Yet conventional policy analysis always describes some parameters as "givens" in order to construct simulations and look at realistic options. If policy analysts can be castigated for being overly conventional in their assumptions, they at least are willing to talk publicly about alternatives and distributional questions. In the political world, we are far away from such discussion. Instead, politicians have offered an exercise in subterfuge and evasion. In aging, the politics of entitlement can be summed up as a strategy of promising to protect existing entitlement programs, then making covert cuts, and attacking one's opponent at every turn.

The problem with conventional politics as it affects aging policy is that any kind of open, rational discourse has virtually been abandoned. Social Security or issues related to entitlement programs are topics simply taboo among serious politicians. This trend started early in the Reagan Administration, in 1982, when it proposed drastic and unpopular cuts in Social Security eligibility. The Democrats responded with outrage and the administration's proposals went down to dramatic defeat. In the presidential election of 1984 Walter Mondale tried to use Social Security as an issue against Reagan. But soon enough the Republicans learned to avoid the issue. The same pattern was repeated in 1986 and 1988. No politician, Democrat or Republican, would say anything that might open up serious debate on the politics of entitlement.

At the same time, during these years, far-reaching changes in the policy on aging were taking place, principally through the budget process. But the changes were made covertly. For example, the 1983 Social Security reform was initiated behind closed doors by a special commission: a favorite if not always successful device on Capitol Hill for handling hot issues.[24] The 1988 Medicare Catastrophic Coverage Act was fashioned by negotiations among staffers and lobbyists; the wider public understood almost nothing about the distributional choices. The bill itself never became an item of debate in the 1988 election.

In contrast to welfare reform or tax reform, which also advanced during these years, policy reform on aging was fashioned outside public scrutiny or debate. It was as if political elites in both parties understood that no serious work could be done if the public looked closely at the distributional issues in entitlement politics. Nor, needless to say, could the framework of entitlement politics itself ever be challenged. In practice, this covert-action approach served to freeze in place the existing structure of entitlements, just as the all-too-public budget deficit served to foreclose serious discussion of major new spending initiatives such as long-term care coverage.

As the decade of the 1980s drew to a close, a strange state of affairs existed. Elites and policy influentials—legislators, journalists, academics, lobbyists—recognized the distributional choices in aging policy and fought on the contested terrain where change was possible. But the public understood little about the technical issues; the gap between mass and elite opinion became wider than ever. Analysts who looked to the future of Medicare, for example, saw bankruptcy threatening by the end of the century. Where would revenues be found, and how could cost containment actually be made to work? No politically feasible answers were apparent. At the same time, advocates for the aging looked at persisting poverty and unmet needs for long-term care; they sought, in vain, for government responses to those needs. They were told that new initiatives (that is, new taxes) were unrealistic. The result on all sides was a kind of policy paralysis that accompanied covert action. In this mood, it is not so strange that the politics of productivity, too, seemed to lie beyond the realm of feasibility. Advocates, like policymakers, were reduced to rear-guard, defensive thinking.

An Impossible Dream? The Politics of Productivity

This chronicle of missed opportunities could be a cause for pessimism. But that attitude would be premature; there are grounds for believing that the "impossible dream" might yet come to pass. In assessing the feasibility of the politics of productivity in aging policy, we need to look beyond the field of aging. If we fail to set our sights in broader terms, we run the risk of believing that the pattern of the past must inevitably be repeated in the future. We should now consider briefly a few policy arenas where calls for reform have come forth, some with success, some with failure.

SUCCESSES

One instructive example is found in the field of educational reform, a persistent topic of controversy in the 1980s.[25] An initial call for reform came in the presidential report called *A Nation at Risk*. That title became a watchword for educational reform designed to counter threats of foreign competition. Since the 1960s, liberals had called for school reform to improve opportunities for the disadvantaged. But the earlier debate had been framed in terms of "quality education for all" and was opposed by the response "but at what cost?" Despite veiled opposition, the older debate had revolved around some common assumptions. On all sides education was taken to be a fixed good, a public entitlement. The policy question was simply how to secure access to more of it and how to pay for what was delivered. This was, in essence, the liberal agenda, in victory or defeat, with familiar landmarks like school integration and student aid.

The new debate on school reform in the 1980s brought a different emphasis: *Quality* education was sought; no longer was access or quantity enough. The new question was framed not in redistributive terms—haves versus have-nots—but in terms of productivity: Will we have an adequately educated work force for the twenty-first century? As the terms of the debate changed, new allies—for example, business leaders—came forward, and new opportunities and risks presented themselves. The politics of productivity had now become an explicit factor in debates about educational reform.

Something very similar happened in the case of welfare reform. The old debate in welfare politics was a familiar one: How much to pay and who should be entitled. Liberals and conservatives lined up on familiar sides: for example, one side attacking "welfare cheats," another demanding "welfare rights."

But in the 1980s, the old terms of debate were recast, above all through state government initiatives. The most famous of these was the Massachusetts Training and Employment Program that blended compulsory training, state-subsidized child care, and aggressive job placement, all designed to move recipients out of welfare. Whether the Massachusetts program and similar initiatives in other states actually lived up to their promise remains a matter of debate. But the whole point was that the welfare discussion had now taken a new turn. No longer was it a matter of redistributive politics alone. Now the politics of productivity set the terms: How best to get welfare recipients into productive employment. In short, the debate moved away from polarizing ideologies and into a more pragmatic key. There were experiments to determine the right mix of child care, job training, and work in order to reduce welfare dependency.

There is no need for us to agree with everything that was put forward under the banner of "school reform" or of "welfare reform" to recognize what was new in both movements. In both cases, the resulting policy mix represented a compromise between long-standing liberal and conservative positions. New constituencies entered the debate. Previous policy paralysis gave way to a new definition of the problem in terms of productivity instead of redistribution. Of course the older debate over access and entitlement, not to mention funding levels, continues to be fought, as it must be. But the terms of the debate have now changed, and this in itself can be counted a measure of success for the politics of productivity.

FAILURES

Unfortunately, there are also prominent examples where the politics of productivity failed to break out of policy gridlock. These examples, too, are instructive.

A familiar case can be found in the field of agricultural policy, in which the United States is annually spending nearly $30 billion on farm subsidies for results that, most analysts agree, are disappointing. At a time when farmers are still paid not to plant crops, agricultural exports have been plummeting and the financial plight of small farmers remains dismal. Here again, there is debate about what to do. The old debate, still very much alive in popular stereotype, was a sentimental one: How do we save the family farm? Unfortunately, the family farm is nearly extinct. But the stereotype helps maintain fixed positions and prop up a subsidy program that frustrates serious change.

The debate might better be framed in terms of how to promote responsible and productive farming, which typically means neither old-style family farms (often inefficient) or new-style agribusiness conglomerates (often environmentally irresponsible). A real debate, for example, might address the question of how to preserve precious topsoil and water resources. Today we have exorbitant subsidies to agribusiness, combined with declining water and soil resources, high energy and resource costs, and falling trade balances in farm products. The environmental impact of farm policies poses serious burdens on future generations—another example of generational inequity. But reforming farm subsidies remains politically impossible.

Still another instance of policy gridlock can be found in the field of international trade policy. The old debate was couched in the familiar terms of an opposition between protectionism versus free trade. In the 1980s getting past the rhetoric and fixed positions proved difficult. Of course, stated policy and actual practice were often at variance, as when the Reagan administration introduced trade quotas (for example, on automobiles) in all but name. In the early 1980s, a brief debate about "industrial policy" flared but was quickly forgotten by both political parties. Yet in defense spending, aerospace, agriculture, and many other industrial sectors we already have evolved a covert but de facto "industrial policy."

The problem with covert policies is that reform is choked off and the status quo is unchallenged. Other alternatives are available. Japan offers a powerful, often-cited example of how flexible trade and industrial policy could in fact promote productivity. But in America the old debate could not get beyond a false opposition between government leadership versus private initiative, between quotas versus competition. As a result, America saw industry after industry—not just shoes or textiles but electronics and computers—fall victim to aggressive practices by trading partners. The real debate should have been around the difficult question of how to deal with the rise of the Pacific Rim Trading States such as Japan, Korea, and Taiwan. The question was not how to enact new quotas—in practice an entitlement to protection—but rather how to mobilize productivity to respond collectively to threats of global competition.

In short, in the case of both agriculture policy and trade policy, powerful vested interests prevented change in response to new economic realities. The result was that, despite the Reagan administration's free-market rhetoric, agricultural subsidies rose to new heights. In trade policies, trade deficits ballooned while back-door quotas were expanded and American firms exported jobs overseas. In both agriculture and trade policy, collective action and innovative policies were thwarted by special interests. Instead of the politics of productivity, the politics of redistribution and subsidy held sway.

Breaking the Gridlock

Whether in success or in failure, the struggle between the politics of entitlement and the politics of productivity takes a clear form and exhibits some structural features that are worth pondering:

1. The politics of productivity promises future benefits, but benefits are often collective goods, widely diffused. In contrast, the politics of entitlement offers tangible benefits to identifiable constituencies. When the benefits are spread widely (for example, Social Security), then the constituency is strong and programs are hard to reform. When the benefits are narrowly directed (for example, trade quotas), then interest groups mobilize intensely to hold on to what they have. Interest-group mobilization, whether narrow or broad-based, presents a problem for political reform and for appeals to productivity.
2. The politics of productivity offers hope of bypassing policy gridlock. On the other hand, the politics of entitlement ends up promising subsidies, paying people who are not in need, and weakening incentives for productivity. Once in place, entitlement programs are notoriously hard to challenge. This is true whether we look at farmers, schools, displaced workers, or welfare recipients. It is also true in the field of aging. We subsidize an inefficient health care system, encourage older people to leave the labor force, and then complain about the high costs of an aging society. Then, when age-based entitlement programs are attacked as "too expensive," the only suggestion is to cut the programs. Advocates for the elderly

predictably respond by defending the status quo, so gridlock continues.

3. The politics of productivity demands a distinctive style of innovation and coalition-building. The key issues involve incentives for change, softening the human costs of economic dislocation, promoting negotiation and consensus-building, and reducing the paralysis of interest-group or ideological conflict. In the case of aging policy, a politics of productivity means thinking about human capital investment on a lifespan basis, as industrial policies in Sweden and Japan have done. Then, for example, when older workers are offered opportunities for retraining and good jobs, they need not oppose automation and labor reforms.
4. In the field of aging, the politics of entitlement remains centered on federal social insurance programs, chiefly Social Security and Medicare, which amount to more than 90 percent of what the federal government spends on aging programs. Throughout the 1980s, these entitlement programs were repeated topics of controversy and reform, with attention focused on areas such as improving target efficiency, addressing issues of equity, and implementing cost-containment steps. But none of these initiatives did anything to reshape incentives for the productivity of older people. This failure must be counted as a major missed opportunity of the 1980s.
5. Policymakers, locked into the redistributive framework, have been drawn ineluctably toward framing a policy on aging in terms of a continuing dilemma: age versus need.[26] But this way of framing the issue has tangible consequences for constituency-building and politics. Framing the issue as need versus age does reflect the diversity of the older population. But it also runs the risk of political divisiveness and, ultimately, the erosion of the legitimacy of universal social insurance programs. Advocates for the elderly thus are left with a troublesome question: How can we maintain broad public support through universal age-based entitlements while also targeting benefits to the least advantaged? There is no easy answer to this dilemma. But one response, surely, could

> be to reframe the agenda in terms of productivity, and not merely entitlement.

One lesson from all the successes and failures of policy reform in the 1980s is the need for a more coherent policy framework, a "road map" to the future. Because we lack any shared image of the future, we end up locked into the present and the past. And incremental reform without a wider framework runs the risk of simply defending the status quo, of missing opportunities and failing to identify ideas that could be the basis for a new politics of aging in the future. The defensive thinking of this decade is a dangerous precedent for the years to come.

Here the political lessons of the 1980s are crucial. What conservatives at the Heritage Foundation and the American Enterprise Institute showed in the 1980s is that ideas count, and they count especially for those who would reshape the political agenda. Policy ideas, such as those centering on productivity urged here, constitute, essentially, the road map to an aging society in the future. But a map by itself will not take us where we need to go. Real political change is needed and that involves constituencies and interest-groups, both those who favor change and those who resist it.

It is instructive that through the politics of productivity the successes of the 1980s came in the human resources field—in education and welfare reform—where productivity concerns began to influence the policy agenda. By contrast, the failures occurred in certain dominant industrial sectors—agriculture and international trade—where it proved impossible to fashion consensus positions to permit trade-offs and significant reform. On the failure side, the causes can be identified, and the presence of powerful interest groups was a decisive factor. In the dominant industrial sectors, key interest groups, such as agribusiness, unions, and multinational corporations, have resisted changing the status quo and have pushed for still more protection and subsidies, often with success. The entitlements of the powerful emerged intact but short-term success bodes ill for the future. Gains for narrow interest groups may turn out to have been purchased at the price of policy paralysis and general decline.[27]

What lessons can we draw here for the field of aging? Are there constituencies in the politics of the aging that would favor a politics of productivity in the future? The answer must be a mixed one, but a cautious optimism seems to be in order. Some constituencies and alliances are certainly foreseeable here: the aging service network itself, the voluntary sector, businesses facing a shortage of workers, higher education looking for nontraditional learners, state governments with the scope to experiment. All these groups have reason to favor a politics of productivity if their own role and interests could be better defined.

A single example can make this point clear. In the case of one major program, the Title V, Senior Community Employment Act, some key interest groups for the elderly (AARP, Green Thumb, NCOA) proved effective in maintaining a sizable program (over $300 million) in the face of attempts by the Reagan administration to cut the program. But in broad economic terms, this program is admittedly only a drop in the bucket. In practice, the Act is little more than a jobs program or a form of patronage for voluntary agencies. But the voluntary sector in coalition with the aging network proved to have an unexpected potency on behalf of productivity.

Similarly, the Job Training and Partnership Act, offering tuition-free educational offerings for older adults, and the much-heralded elimination of mandatory retirement are related. But serious impact is yet to be seen on income, employment, retraining, or on the dominant practices of work and retirement in American life. None of these programs has been promoted or legitimated in terms of any wider vision of productivity by older people. All are instructive for how programs might be fashioned in the future, however. Until a politics of productivity becomes part of the agenda of mainstream business, labor, education, and government, we will fail to make use of the enlarged productive capability of America's older population, now ignored by the practices of our dominant institutions.

Yet if we believe both in incremental politics and a positive vision of the future, then we will need to make use of all the lessons from these programs and their constituencies. The lessons will help fashion a practical politics of productivity as it begins to inch its way into the public agenda. Examples are few but they are tangible and so furnish a basis for action and advocacy. But along with political *action*, there is an equally important need for political *thinking* framed in terms of productivity. And failing to respond to the diversity and the strength of America's aging population means failing to use the resources that lie in our midst. That failure is like starvation in the midst of plenty: a contradiction to be pondered and, finally, a challenge for collective action. But action will not come without a new vision. The vision is that an aging society need not be a prescription for zero-sum politics. With political will, it could be an opportunity for abundance of life for all generations.

Notes

1. Butler, R. *Productive Aging*. New York: Springer, 1985.
2. Committee on an Aging Society. *Productive Roles in an Older Society*. Washington, D.C.: National Academy Press, 1986.
3. Phillipson, C., M. Bernard, and P. Strong. (Eds.). *Dependency and Independency in Old Age: Theoretical Perspectives and Policy Alternatives*. London: Croom Helm, 1986.
4. Bass, A. "Symposium on tomorrow's able elderly: Implications for policy and practice." *The Gerontologist* 27, 4 (1987): 403–404.
5. Morris, R.A. and S.A. Bass (Eds.). *Retirement Reconsidered: Economic and Social Roles for Older People*. New York: Springer, 1988.
6. Kuttner, R. *The Economic Illusion: False Choices between Prosperity and Justice*. Boston: Houghton Mifflin, 1984.
7. Ferguson, T. and J. Rogers. *Right Turn: The Decline of the Democrats and the Future of American Politics*. New York: Hill and Wang, 1987.
8. Longman, P. *Born to Pay: The New Politics of Aging in America*. Boston: Houghton Mifflin, 1987.
9. Marmor, T.R. and J.L. Mashaw (Eds.). *Social Security: Beyond the Rhetoric of Crisis*. Princeton, N.J.: Princeton University Press, 1988.
10. Moody, H.R. "The contradictions of an aging society: From zero sum to productive society." In Morris and Bass (Eds.). *Retirement Reconsidered*. New York: Springer, 1988.
11. Kingson, E.R., B.A. Hirshorn, and J.M. Cornman. *Ties That Bind: The Interdependence of Generations*. Washington, D.C.: Seven Locks Press, 1986.
12. Torres-Gil, F. "The politics of catastrophic and long-term care coverage." *Journal of Aging Policy* 1, 1, 1989.
13. Moody, H.R. *Abundance of Life: Human Development Policies for an Aging Society*. New York: Columbia University Press, 1988.

14. Heller, P.S. *Aging and Social Expenditure in the Major Industrial Countries, 1980-2025*, IMF Occasional Paper No. 47. Washington, D.C.: International Monetary Fund, 1986.

15. Pifer, A. and L. Bronte (Eds.). *Our Aging Society: Paradox and Promise*. New York: Norton, 1986.

16. Clark, W.F. *Old and Poor*. Lexington, Mass.: Lexington Books, 1988.

17. Kuttner, R. *The Life of the Party: Democratic Prospects in 1988 and Beyond*. New York: Viking, 1988.

18. Thurow, L.C. *The Zero-Sum Society*. New York: Basic Books, 1980.

19. Sandell, S.H. (Ed.). *The Problem Isn't Age: Work and Older Americans*. New York: Praeger, 1987.

20. Kalish, R.A. "The new ageism and the failure models: A polemic." *The Gerontologist* 19 (1979): 398–402.

21. Aaron, H., B. Bosworth, and G. Burtless. *Can America Afford to Grow Old?*. Washington, D.C.: Brookings Institution, 1989.

22. Iler, P. and W. Laure. *Graying of the National Budget: The Year 2020*. American Statistical Association Proceedings, 1984.

23. Graebner, W. *A History of Retirement*. New Haven, Conn.: Yale University Press, 1980.

24. Light, P. *Artful Work: The Politics of Social Security Reform*. New York: Random House, 1985.

25. Gross, B. and R. Gross. *The Great School Debate*. New York: Simon and Schuster, 1985.

26. Neugarten, B. (Ed.). *Age or Need?*, Beverly Hills, Calif.: SAGE, 1982.

27. Olson, M. *The Rise and Fall of Nations: Economic Growth, Stagflation, and Social Rigidities*. New Haven, Conn.: Yale University Press, 1982.

CHAPTER SIX

Elder Leadership for a Diverse America

FERNANDO M. TORRES-GIL AND MIMI KMET

The American social and political profile is in a constant state of change, and by the next century, this continuing diversification will have changed the face of the U.S. population from what it is today. It is a demographic revolution that spans all generations. As previous chapters of this book have made clear, the group called "the elderly" is heterogeneous and can no longer be considered a single group based on age alone. The challenge we now face lies in how we respond to the social, economic, and political pressures brought about by our ever-changing American profile. The choices we make today will determine whether we and our children will enjoy a prosperous and contented old age tomorrow.

But will we make the policy and political decisions today to prepare us for a diverse aging society tomorrow? Do we have the political will to make hard decisions about reforming public benefits and programs, providing access to low-income and disadvantaged elderly, promoting productivity among elders, and reversing the adverse effects of a capitalist free-market economy? Will we invest in educating and training a young population to be able and willing to provide public support for an older population? The political climate of the 1980s and early 1990s suggests that we are not ready to make those difficult political choices—that the electorate lacks the will and the leadership to look ahead and plan for tomorrow. This period suggests that interest groups—particularly those representing large constituencies such as women and minorities, as well as those advocating gun control and abortion rights—may be more concerned with their own issues than in the population changes confronting the nation.

The elderly in particular are seen by some as a narrow and selfish interest group intent on protecting their vast public benefits and services, even while other groups such as minorities and children, become poorer. Their political clout, including their higher voting rates, is viewed as a barrier to meaningful political change. On the contrary, it is because of that political leverage that the elderly are in the best position to provide the political leadership necessary for the future.

Older persons are in fact concerned with the welfare of their children and grandchildren. A lifetime of both adversity and contributions to the nation gives them unique wisdom and interest in supporting a diverse aging society. But, as for any group, encouraging elders to lead in this area requires an understanding of why it is in their own self-interest to champion those changes that relieve the pressure of a diverse population. What are those pressures and what is it about diversity that makes social and political change compelling? Why is it in the self-interest of the elderly and the nation for older persons to exercise leadership? What are the consequences of not preparing now for a diverse aging population?

Not since the early days of this century have we faced such pressures to plan for the long term. This time, however, the pressures are based not on our earlier phenomena of immigration, industrialization, and technological innovations, but rather on the aging phenomenon—the growing numbers of our older persons and the aging of the society as a whole.

The impact that the diversification of the United States has on aging goes beyond providing social and public benefits to senior citizens; it also raises issues of equity, of economic and political stability, and of preparing for the twenty-first century.

The Social and Demographic Mandate

The growing diversity of the aged population will affect us all. We can no longer assume that all older persons have the same needs and will support the same issues; in fact, we never could. Future generations of older persons will be radically different from today's elderly, according to Cynthia Taeuber (Chapter 1). Four-generation households, increasing numbers of racial and minority groups, changes in the roles of women, differences in who is poor, and new life-styles are a few examples of what is to come.

The aged population will comprise a large proportion of the U.S. population by the year 2010. Up to one-quarter of our people will be older than 60 years of age. And what unites older persons today—support for Social Security and Medicare—may break down to alliances based more on class, race, and social circumstances. Old age may no longer hold the status it once held.

This increasingly heterogeneous aged population will place tremendous demands on society's fiscal resources, particularly when that group has the potential for tremendous political influence. Higher life expectancies and a smaller youth population will place a premium on labor force productivity. And the increasing numbers of minorities—especially those in the labor force—will push our tolerance for racial and ethnic diversity to its limits. Other pressures will be the continued departure of women from traditional roles in the home and the changes in life-styles. Demands will be placed on the state, because of these pressures, to supplant personal responsibility.

To cope with an aged society now requires us to move beyond our interest in traditional senior citizen issues such as public benefits, interest group politics, leisure, and retirement. It requires a broader focus on economics, politics, ideology, and the impact of aging on the entire population, young and old.

As individuals, we have a personal stake. Whether to have children today confronts baby boomers anxious to prepare for their future old age. Maintaining sufficient reserves in the Social Security system is of prime importance to both older persons receiving benefits and younger workers paying increasingly high taxes. Reversing the economic and international disadvantages faced by American industry is inextricably tied with a declining work force and growing numbers of retirees. And tough decisions necessary to allocate federal and state dollars in a time of a huge federal deficit are made tougher by the fear elected officials have of alienating a politically potent elder lobby.

Why is it that we need to understand the forces of this demographic revolution and look beyond our own immediate self-interest?

The United States is at a turning point—a milestone in its development, where the decisions and actions taken in the 1990s will determine whether the first half of the next century will see a decline in American influence and prosperity or a resurgence in its national fortunes. We have faced these crossroads before. The periods immediately after the American Revolution and the Civil War saw major decisions and adaptations leading to national prominence. The social and political revolution during the Great Depression and World War II created the conditions for affluence and international prominence. In the same manner, the decisions made by both the electorate and the elected in the 1990s will affect how we deal with the growing numbers of elderly of the next century.

We face this situation for several reasons. The United States is shifting from an industrial base to a technological economy at the same time that other nations are prospering. We are now confronting a lack of investment in our physical and social infrastructures—roads, buildings, airports and health, education, research. And this is occurring during the same time that the American profile is changing.

We can respond successfully if we see diversity as a challenge and an opportunity for national prosperity. That challenge lies in seeing older persons as resources and permitting greater opportunities for minorities and women. The elderly have a unique mission in forcing the political system to respond to those needs.

The Future and the New Elderly

Exactly what type of future awaits us? The most dramatic growth of older persons will begin, as noted earlier, around 2010, when the baby-boom generation—that large post-World War II population born between 1946 and 1964—begins to retire. That is only two decades away—by then most of us reading this chapter will still be alive.

By 2030, 20 percent of the population may be 65 years of age and older. By 2010, it is expected that one-third will be between 55 and 75 years of age. With the youth population on the decline and the elderly on the rise, dependency ratios will continue to narrow, with more elderly depending on a smaller labor force. If current retirement patterns continue, with a trend toward earlier retirement, we will have a huge population of retirees on our hands in the next century.

Aging and retirement in 2010 and beyond can be something to look forward to if

- those retirees have adequate retirement income;
- they are reasonably healthy, and when sick, have access to affordable and quality health care;
- housing is affordable and comfortable; and
- their communities are safe.

That scenario, which we all aspire to, assumes that

- affordable housing will be available;
- crime and drugs will be less serious problems than they are today;
- pension and retirement programs will remain solvent and will not be eroded by inflation;
- Medicare and Medicaid will remain well funded, or if in another guise, will provide basic health care;
- scientific progress will be made to combat AIDS, Alzheimer's disease, arthritis, and other forms of premature chronic illnesses; and
- older persons will have access to family- and community-based care as they become dependent.

That future is what we want for our children and our grandchildren. What parents and grandparents want is to know that future generations will have a good life throughout old age. Positive expectations of the next century affect our attitudes today. Whether the world will be safe tomorrow may affect, though not always consciously, whether young persons today decide to have children. And if we feel our economy and society are strong and will remain intact for generations to come, we are more likely to save, invest, and pass on what we have accumulated to our heirs.

Today's senior citizens know the importance of hope and expectations. They suffered and worked hard to overcome the hardships of the 1930s in the belief that their children would have a better life. They maintained their basic belief that the foundations of the nation were strong, that people were essentially good, and that justice would prevail. World War II strengthened that belief in the inherent rightness of this nation. The ability of government, individuals, and society to come together and pursue a common goal—the defeat of fascism to make the world safer for future generations—was significant. And through the 1950s, 1960s, and 1970s, that belief prevailed and the resultant prosperity and material progress of the nation confirmed people's decisions to have children.

Older Americans today want that same optimism and hope to work for their children and grandchildren. They want younger persons to know that if they work hard, sacrifice, and share, life will be better for them and their country. A better society and a better old age for future generations remains the fundamental hope of today's older population.

The outcome of those aspirations is predicated on the same factors that faced Americans in the 1920s, 1930s, and 1940s:

- a world safe from war and totalitarianism;
- the education of young people;
- an expanding economy that benefits all persons;
- successful integration of new nationalities and minorities of long duration; and
- a safe environment.

Through the early part of this century, democracy overcame the threat of authoritarian regimes, the nation invested tremendous resources to educate its young, the economy became stronger after the Depression and World War II, the gaps between the rich and poor narrowed, civil rights advanced, and people felt reasonably safe in their homes and neighborhoods.

But today, there are warning signs that the progress of the previous four decades may be reversed—signs that the sacrifice and preparation necessary to prepare for the future may not be taking place. Despite the relative progress of the 1980s—wherein peace and prosperity appeared to be the mode, inflation was kept under control, unemployment was reasonably low, there were no major wars, and the public held a relatively high regard for its political institutions—undercurrents of instability, problems, and turmoil festered and created pressures for change.

Social and Economic Disruptions

The United States has undergone rapid transformation throughout its existence. As a largely agrarian, rural society, then an industrialized world power, and now a highly technological international competitor, the United States has had to adapt to tremendous external and internal pressures. By and large, we have done so successfully.

We avoided the worst excesses of industrialization in the nineteenth century, those that led to revolutions in other nations. We held together and matured as a nation after the Civil War. The recessions and economic disruptions imposed by the railroad, oil, and steel monopolies of the early part of this century were brought under control by government intervention and antitrust legislation. The nation responded collectively to the travails of the Great Depression, World War II, and the Korean War. It is now coming to grips with the aftermath of the Civil Rights Era and the Vietnam War.

The new pressures we face are no less significant than those we have faced in the last one hundred years. They include responding to the computer age, the prevalence of a nuclear arms race, a move toward decentralized government, and a changing world economy.

The Demographic Revolution

Perhaps no other change is as visible and omnipresent now as the demographic revolution. The forces of this revolution, Taeuber says, are increased longevity, growing numbers of older persons, and declining numbers of younger persons.

These forces will fundamentally alter how we live our lives. Living longer requires a shift in our attitudes about the meaning of "old age." Already we see a shift in how we measure middle age—it is now assumed to begin in one's forties instead of one's thirties. Young people now marry and have children later in life. People in their sixties increasingly are seen as relatively young, compared with earlier generations of older persons. All of these changes are affecting public policies: the Social Security Amendments of 1983 will eventually raise the eligibility age for receipt of full benefits to 67. We can expect public and private pensions to follow suit.

The demographic revolution also involves the feminization of aging, with a continuing gap in the life expectancies of men and women. Issues affecting older women will become critical for an older society where women outlive men by up to seven years. The decline in fertility rates and the resulting fewer children will mean a smaller yet much-needed labor force.[1]

The aging of the baby-boom generation will be our biggest demographic change and will produce our largest group of elders, starting around 2010. They will cause dramatic changes in dependency ratios. In the fifteen years between 2010 and 2025, the working-age population will decline by as much as 12 million, while the elderly population will grow from 42 million to 62 million.[2] Senior boomers will rely on that declining labor force for the taxes to pay their benefits. That smaller labor force, however, may be able to shoulder that responsibility only if individual productivity increases (that is, through labor saving devices, improved skills), we make better use of minorities (through education and job training), and we encourage retirees to re-enter the work force.

Ethnic Diversity

The dramatic ethnic diversification we are seeing now is not unlike that which occurred in the last century. The mid-nineteenth century saw a tremendous immigration of ethnic groups that now make up the "American" character: Irish, Italians, Scandinavians, Slavs, Anglo Saxons.[3] Those groups and later groups from southern and eastern Europe were vital to America's expansion and industrialization. Although many people faced tremendous discrimination and exploitation, they eventually were accepted and acculturated into American life.

This century is facing a similar situation with the rapid migration and growth of peoples from the Third World: those from Africa, the Caribbean, Latin America, and the Pacific Basin. Asians and Pacific Islanders, Hispanics, and, to a lesser extent, blacks from the Caribbean and Africa will fundamentally alter the American profile. In many parts of the country, especially California, Florida, New York, and areas of the Great Lakes region, those groups are becoming a majority population.[4]

If we can be sure that assimilation will work for them as it did for earlier immigrant groups, then their presence might not be an overriding issue. But that is not the case. Hispanics and Asians in particular are not assimilating as rapidly as earlier groups did. Their languages, cultures, and traditions remain, and actually influence popular culture. Ease of communications and transportation makes it possible for them to maintain links with their countries of origin, unlike immigrant groups of the last century.

More important, their numbers are growing faster than the general population. On the average, they have more children than the majority white population.[5] That fact, combined with their continuing immigration, ensures their large populations here. Early in the next century, Hispanics, Asians, and other immigrant groups, including white ethnics such as Armenians and Russians, will overshadow the largely white, English-speaking descendants of earlier immigrant groups.

The Permanency of an Underclass

Hidden from the apparent affluence of the 1980s is one of the more disturbing pressures facing this country: the growth of a poor, disenfranchised population that does not progress. For example, throughout the 1980s the American economy in general enjoyed a sustained recovery, with real per capita income increasing 16.2 percent from 1982 to 1987. Yet from 1973 to 1986, the real median income for young families headed by someone aged 20 to 24 dropped by 27 percent—an amount equal to the drop in personal income during the Great Depression.[6] And in the period from 1973 to 1986, real median income dropped 40 percent for young black families, 19 percent for white families, and 18 percent for Hispanic families.[7]

It has always been a general rule that in American democracy all immigrant groups, regardless of race, ethnicity, or language, will eventually assimilate and be upwardly mobile. With the exception of small, isolated pockets of people, such as poor Appalachian whites, every such group in the last century has become middle class. But for the first time, we may now have large numbers of certain racial and ethnic peoples who will spend generations locked in poverty and hopelessness.

Nothing illustrates this scenario more clearly than the plight of innercity blacks. In many major metropolitan areas of the United States, large populations of blacks, as well as increasing numbers of Hispanics and Asians, are poor, illiterate, unemployed, and locked in a cycle of violence and poverty. In some ways, sections of Detroit, New York, Miami, Los Angeles, and Chicago now appear more like Third World than First World cities.

Irrespective of political parties, government and society have failed to provide the necessary educational, employment, and material resources for certain groups. In turn, they have failed to develop the family and social institutions that foster upward mobility. The prevalence of teenage pregnancy, unemployed youth, drugs, and violence, and the total insecurity of those neighborhoods, has created unlivable environments that many citizens fear to enter.

The Changing World Economy

Along with the factors of the demographic revolution, ethnic diversification, and the underclass is another phenomenon not faced since World War II: a changing world economy wherein the United States must compete with other nations for military and economic primacy.

The United States is no longer the dominant military and economic power in the world. It cannot assume its economy will automatically expand, because it must now compete with others, particularly Europe and the Pacific Basin nations, for exports and imports.[8] The watchwords for the 1980s have been "foreign competition" and "productivity"—beating other nations by enhancing productivity at home. But productivity at home relies on a trained work force, efficient industries, and investments in plants, capital, and people. We are in the latter part of the twentieth century where we were in the 1930s and 1940s: forced to re-evaluate our industrial and economic base to find out what works and what does not, to reinvest in plants and machinery, and to ensure that our labor force has the education and skills to adapt to changing technologies.

And we have mishandled our economic changes. Borrowing from abroad to finance borrowing and spending at home has made us the world's largest debtor nation. The continuing federal deficit restricts our ability to invest in research and industry. Fears about imports create a garrison protectionism that further erodes markets for our goods. Peterson[9] refers to the mounting trade deficit and federal deficit as the "Argentining of America," because we refuse to restrict borrowing and spending and to increase internal savings and investments. Inevitably, such practices will lead to a decline in the standard of living for all of us.

Our ability to compete in international commerce will depend on how well we understand that competition and how well we adjust to it.

What does this economic scenario mean to the average person? What does it mean to the elderly? Today's elderly are beneficiaries of our economic success and the international prominence we have enjoyed over the last forty years. That success has allowed our economy to expand and provide the fiscal resources to pay for public entitlements. A rising standard of living meant that individuals were more willing than previously to pay taxes for public services and public investments such as roads, education, and employment. Economic success has also been reflected in a higher level of retirement income from private pension plans.

Retirement security or the lack of it and the standard of living of tomorrow's elderly—especially those retiring after 2010—will be determined largely by our economic performance in the next twenty to thirty years. If we adjust and compete successfully with other nations, if our work force is capable of working in the new industries and with new skills, then we can expect continuing productivity and economic expansion. That will provide the public resources needed to pay for benefits and services. If we are not successful, then tomorrow's elderly may face a bleak future.

Environmental Prospects

Final factors that will determine how today's young people fare in their old age include environmental issues such as preservation of natural resources and controlling toxic and chemical dangers. The importance of maintaining healthy diets and life-styles and avoiding nuclear and chemical wars is obvious. Some of the environmental dangers are controllable. Safeguarding our forests, beaches, and water are well within our means. Acid rain, polluted lakes and rivers, eroding beaches, and "greenhouse" effects on the planet illustrate the man-made dangers we create when we are unwilling to safeguard our environment. Aging will not be successful, no matter how well we handle our economy, if our environment is damaged.

Additionally, gains in life expectancy require that we take better care of our bodies. Good mental health, exercise, and diet have a direct relationship to our physical health in old age. Avoiding cigarettes and drugs and using a seat belt also increase the chances that we will live to an old age.

Scenarios

Demographic changes, ethnic and racial diversity, an economic underclass, a changing world economy, and our environment are all elements or factors that will critically affect successful aging and our lives in the early part of the next century. How we respond to these factors constitutes some of the major pressures facing American society. But why should today's elderly care about the next century? Why should they worry about the environment, the needs of new ethnic and racial groups, or the changing world economy, especially if they are enjoying a comfortable retirement and their children are relatively well off?

For several reasons: Parents care about their children, and grandparents care about their grandchildren. Today's older people sacrificed and worked hard to give their offspring a good life. But that life-style of work and preparation for the future may be threatened, and their offspring may find their own retirement less secure. To guarantee that it is at least as enjoyable as it might be today, those pressures must be addressed. In addition, today's retirees are likely to live into their eighties and nineties, and many will be alive when their children begin to retire. Elderly parents with elderly children will become more commonplace. Whatever happens at the turn of the century will happen to most of the elderly now with us. For that reason, today's elderly have a personal stake in the pressures facing our society into the next century.

What if we do not address today the social and economic pressures now facing us? What if we are not successful at integrating minority groups? What if the underclass grows and major cities continue to become unlivable? What if we do not expand the economy or protect the environment?

The answer is relatively clear, although the solutions are complex. If we do nothing between now and the year 2010, and if current social, economic, and political trends continue, aging in the next century will not be pleasant. We will have many more poor persons, a breakdown of our transportation and public infrastructures (for example, bridges falling down, inadequate sewer capacity), growing numbers of resentful and politically disenfranchised groups (minorities, young persons, older women, the disabled), a country characterized by division and conflict, and a paralyzed political system torn between competing interest groups.

For example, if current trends continue through the year 2010, the elderly population will rely heavily on the labor force's ability and willingness to be productive and pay the taxes necessary to support public benefits and programs. If today's population continues to save at a low rate, and pension and retirement programs terminate because of bankruptcies caused by foreign competition, older persons will be forced to rely heavily on Social Security as a safety net, creating pressure to increase taxes. The huge Social Security surplus of today will be of small consequence when the Treasury notes holding the surplus come due and taxes are raised to repay Social Security. And older persons who used drugs or alcohol in their youth or jeopardized their physical health in other ways will create a greater strain on health services. These pressures, along with greater numbers of older persons with few or no children on whom they might depend, will create a demand for more social and long-term-care services.

At the other end of the age spectrum, the labor force of the next century will be heavily composed of Hispanic, black, and certain immigrant groups brought in as guest workers. That labor force will reveal the effects of a decline in quality public education, especially at the primary and secondary levels. Large numbers of workers will be illiterate and unable to cope with the technology of the next century. Greater numbers will be permanently underemployed and unemployed. Businesses will continue to move abroad, where a more complacent, stable work force will accept lower wages.

Those members of the U.S. labor force earning high wages may resist tax increases. The decline of America, already popularized among opinion writers, will achieve its full bloom around that time.

We will find that many central cities will become unlivable—full of crime, congestion, and pollution. The gaps between the haves and have nots within them will widen. Entire sections will be walled compounds of disenchanted and disenfranchised poor persons. America's superb highway, railroad, bridge, water, and sewage systems will be in severe disrepair. Many sections of the country will face polluted water and rivers, contaminated farmlands, and eroding beaches and ports.

This scenario paints a bleak picture facing those people who plan to retire around 2010 and enjoy the security of pensions, decent neighborhoods, and a prosperous America. Instead, they may find themselves, if they are lucky, moving to retirement communities protected by walls and barbed wire or placed in remote areas far from dangerous metropolitan communities. The less fortunate will be forced to deal with dangerous streets, rationed health and human services, and a polyglot population of resentful and conflicting communities. America will become a nation of individuals concerned with their own security and needs—a society of people surviving for the moment, fearful and suspicious, out to protect only themselves and their families. Our sense of nationhood and national community will be severely threatened.

Evidence of these trends already exists to a limited extent. Blacks have a high underemployment rate, and Hispanics have close to a 50 percent school-drop-out rate. Our nation's physical infrastructure already faces serious disrepair, while air pollution and toxic damage to groundwater and radioactive contamination have already surfaced. Many people pay more in Social Security taxes than they do in income taxes, and the nation's deficit continues to be an intractable problem while the public refuses to increase taxes to lower it.

A more positive scenario, in which many of these problems can be avoided, is to change public policies so as to encourage a more active and educated retiree population to re-enter the work force, thus contributing their productivity and reducing pressure on public entitlement programs. A major investment in public education and training programs, particularly in urban areas, would produce a skilled, disciplined labor force that could compete with other nations. Encouraging immigration and including all racial and ethnic groups into mainstream society would provide a young, stable work force that is a major investment draw for foreign companies. Baby boomers in their old age would then find that the economy is prosperous, minorities and younger workers are highly valued, the investments in the 1990s and the early twenty-first century are paying off, and their own numbers have created a huge consumer market that enhances the economy.

We are seeing signs of movement in that direction. In major cities such as Los Angeles, San Francisco, Baltimore, and Boston, corporations are adopting inner-city schools to ensure that their students receive skilled training and are guaranteed jobs. In states such as California, citizens have voted for increased taxes and bond measures to improve public education and health programs. The shortage of teachers is encouraging some retirees to return to the classroom.

What more can be done to minimize the bleaker scenario and enhance a more optimistic one? What should be done to make a better world for tomorrow's society? And why are the elderly best positioned to provide that leadership?

Values and Goals for the 1990s

Before identifying the necessary actions and discussing the potential for elder leadership, we must adopt some fundamental goals and values.

UNDERSTANDING AND ACCEPTING CHANGE

Change is inevitable. America's strength lies in its ability to adapt and respond to change. How we respond to the changes outlined so far will affect our future. Ignoring societal trends and promoting the status quo will bring conflict later on. Our society's individualism is a virtue, but taken to the extreme, it leads to selfishness and isolation. Coming together to discuss and debate what is happening in our country and planning for political and social actions will bring results.

RE-ESTABLISHING A SENSE OF COMMUNITY

Despite our infatuation with individualism, we have maintained a sense of community. Patriotism, loyalty, and pride are statements of our American community. We do come together as a people in times of crisis. The lack of serious religious and ethnic strife, so prevalent in other countries, is a sure sign that we see ourselves first as Americans and second as members of interest groups. Our belief in assimilation, held strongly by all immigrant and ethnic groups, attests to our ability to come together as one. Re-establishing this sense of community and recognizing that all persons—whether young minorities, recent immigrants, the handicapped, or the elderly—are central to a sense of community, will contribute to a greater America.

PUBLIC SACRIFICES AND INVESTMENT OF RESOURCES

Public sacrifices and investment of resources are essential in planning for the future. Those sacrifices, if borne by all, need not be onerous. They involve community action, volunteerism, the willingness to raise taxes when necessary, and to accept compromises, even if that means modifying some public benefits. Our resources need to be invested in the education of young persons; for example, investing in inner-city schools to ensure that blacks and Hispanics will be productive members of the labor force. Investments in research and small businesses will better prepare us for foreign competition. And our physical infrastructure needs attention.

LEADERSHIP AND POLITICAL ALLIANCES

We must develop political leadership that looks ahead and faces hard choices, leadership that does not cater to superficial fads or public whims and is less concerned about political power and longevity in office than in educating the public. In recent years we have avoided economic reality by fixating on public and private scandals and political trivia. Facing this reality requires that we shift our political alliances away from single-interest issues. The elderly are key to developing alliances with minorities, young persons, single parents, and political leaders who are willing to plan ahead and respond to change.

REFRAMING IDEOLOGIC VALUES

Responding to change and preparing for an aging society requires a move away from simple ideologic labels. The terms "Liberal" and "Conservative" are becoming increasingly meaningless at best and harmful at worst. Adopting pragmatic solutions for our problems and determining what works, as did Roosevelt in the 1930s and Eisenhower in the 1950s, should be our first priority.

Responding to the Challenge: Elder Leadership

Today's senior citizens hold the key to a positive future and to the promotion of these values and goals. Older persons are a potent political force, with a voting power greater than any other age group. In 1986, more than 29 million (16 percent) of the 178 million Americans of voting age were 65 and older. One of every five persons (21 percent) who reported voting in that year's presidential election was an older person.[10] Persons in the 55 to 64 and 65 to 74 age groups participate more in elections than other age groups. That participation varies by gender and race. Older men are more likely to vote than older women, and older whites are more likely to vote than older blacks and Hispanics.[11] But even within black and Hispanic populations the elderly are more likely to vote than younger minorities.[12]

However, the elderly are not a political bloc. As Robert Binstock has explained in Chapter 3, older persons have diverse opinions and loyalties that transcend their political role as older persons. Where their interests converge and the electorate at large has little interest, older persons can sway an election. For example, during the 1988 election primary, older persons played a pivotal role. Of those people voting on "super Tuesday," when southern states were selecting presidential candidates, almost 31 percent were 60 and older, even though that age group accounted for only about 22 percent of the voting-age population.[13] In Florida, 40 percent of the Democratic-primary voters were 60 years or older. The increasing numbers of older persons in the early part of the next century will heighten the electoral clout of the elderly. As these data indicate, older persons represent leadership whose political leverage can help reverse the disturbing trends facing the United States today. It will be through their efforts that reforms can and must occur.

Having lived long and fruitful lives, older people also have the wisdom and the experience to know why and when reforms require public sacrifice and commitment. Their sacrifices and commitments during the 1930s, 1940s, and 1950s have made today's society prosperous and, in fact, the leaders of that period are now today's elders. They intuitively understand that certain investments and sacrifices will be required during the 1990s to prepare for the next century. And, as important, they have the political muscle to force changes. Politicians fear their voting strength, and government responds to their demands.

Unfortunately, the elderly have been portrayed lately as a selfish interest group, concerned only with the preservation of their benefits and entitlements and not with the increased poverty facing children or the damage wrought by huge federal deficits. As we have mentioned earlier in this book, newspaper and magazine articles have come to refer to the "conflict between generations," "the greedy elderly" and "age wars."[14] Chakravarty and Weisman,[15] for example, have argued that the elderly are "consuming our children" through a massive redistribution of wealth from the 1950s through the 1980s, through increased Social Security benefits, and through inflationary increases in real estate and home equity.

The irony is that today's elderly have probably given more to our country than any generation currently alive. But, fair or not, a negative picture of the elderly clouds the public's perception of senior citizens as a political force. And the specter of intergenerational conflict is a possibility if we allow the interests of the elderly to be pitted against the needs of younger persons and the poor. The pressures facing a diverse aging America raise that possibility and may create tensions between groups competing for scarce public resources. Older Americans can help reverse this negative perception and ameliorate the situation by working now to help relieve the pressures facing American society.

Reinvesting in America: The Best Is Yet to Come

Talking about the future and speculating about things to come too easily leads to either "doom and gloom" forecasts or rosy, "avoid bad news" discussions. Americans hate the former, and politicians emphasize the latter. Because we hate bad news, we tend to listen to those who give us easy and painless prescriptions. As Americans, we are nurtured and socialized to believe in the inevitability of American greatness and prowess—we are the best, and all other nations must be compared to us.

The reality is that we have been the best but we are in danger of losing that which has made us great. Civic responsibility, sharing ideas and common goals, looking ahead and supporting certain leaders who are willing to tell us what is necessary to improve are hallmarks of past greatness. Today's senior citizens remember those leaders—Presidents Franklin Roosevelt, Harry Truman, and Dwight Eisenhower. We have faced periods of decline as a nation, and we have responded with midcourse corrections.

The bad news is that we face serious decline in our society if we fail to look ahead to correct the pressures of today. The good news is that, with the elderly in the lead, the best is yet to come.

The best is yet to come because we have inherent strengths that no other nation possesses. For example, Kotkin and Kishimoto[16] argue that we maintain latent power. Our entrepreneurship and small business productivity are unmatched anywhere in the world. We possess natural resources (land, minerals, oil) that other nations lack. In addition, we continue to welcome immigrants from other nations. Much of the industrialized world restricts immigration; and much of it—Japan and Germany, for example—will face labor shortages as the population becomes older. But the United States continues to attract industrious individuals from other countries—Latinos, Asians, Europeans, Canadians—who contribute their energies and talents and ensure a steady labor pool. The energies of minorities as well as older persons represent a vast untapped source of productivity—if we use them wisely. In short, we have what it takes to regain our dominance and power. And we must begin now to take the appropriate steps toward that goal.

The number one priority is investment: in educating and training the work force of tomorrow, in particular young minorities who are most likely to be left behind but upon whom we will rely for increased productivity; in good health care and adequate shelter for all persons so that we erase the stigma of being the last industrialized nation to ensure its citizenry of basic health care and housing; and in our deteriorating physical infrastructure—our bridges, highways, and industries. Investment also implies savings—increasing our net savings rates and reducing borrowing from foreign countries and through credit cards and installment payments.

We must reshift federal resources away from foreign and domestic debt payments to activities that reinvest in the American economy. Reducing our trade and federal deficits remains a critical priority if we are to eliminate our debtor status and increase the value of the American dollar.

Forcing these changes on the political system requires grassroots action. The elderly are best positioned for that action, and politicians will act if they are pressured by grassroots organizations into doing so. We have seen seniors wielding such power in the 1980s; their basic programs were preserved while many others were cut severely. But if senior citizens agree with the need to invest for the long term, if they agree that the tremendous diversity facing America creates pressure for change, and if they agree that America is headed for a period of decline unless it responds to that pressure, then they must also confront difficult political issues.

An inescapable issue, according to Robert Binstock, is the fact that public benefits and services for older persons have done little to reach those who are most in need. Although poverty among the elderly has been substantially reduced in recent years, it is still high among minorities, women, the frail elderly, and those living in rural areas. To ensure that all older persons benefit from existing entitlement programs, they—and we—must look at how eligibility and benefits are calculated and dispersed, especially if we assume that reduction of the federal and trade deficits requires financial sacrifices.

The power of the elderly lobby, which is primarily white and comprises the "highly articulate and politically aware middle class,"[17] must be rechanneled. A backlash against the perceived narrowness and self-interest of this group is occurring. Many elected officials and some segments of the public feel that the elderly are concerned only with their own entitlements and not about the poor elderly or larger economic needs. There is some validity to this perception. As previously touched on, the means-tested poverty programs such as Aid to Families with Dependent Children, Supplementary Security Income, and Medicaid suffered heavy cutbacks in the 1980s, while Social Security, Medicare, and the Older Americans Act actually grew. The intense opposition by middle-income older persons to the Medicare Catastrophic Coverage Act because it required a supplemental premium for the more affluent elderly heightened the perception that these people were concerned only with their own health and retirement benefits.

Older persons are in a unique position to change this thinking, by rechanneling their advocating and lobbying power from special interest issues toward policies and programs that will benefit diverse future generations. Cole argues for "rebuilding the moral economy of an extended life course" and forging "a new sense of the meaning and purposes of the last half of life."[18] He sees a "resurgence of the view that old age is a period of unique capacity for wisdom, for understanding the experiences of a lifetime and for giving assistance and advice to the young."[19] Peterson[20] describes "the indissoluble bond between the economic behavior of one decade or generation and the economic well-being of the next decade or generation"[21] and argues that "true vision requires the forging of a farsighted and realistic connection between our present and our future."[22]

Who better than the politically sophisticated elderly to forge that vision, to argue for the need to invest for the long term? Who better to lobby and fight for increased funding for education and health care, and for increased revenues to reduce the federal deficit, which, if left unattended, will be the fiscal legacy for their children and grandchildren? Who better than the influential aging organizations to develop alliances with groups representing minorities and children to fight for prenatal programs and day care for single mothers? And who is in the best position to force elected officials at the state and federal levels to talk about the hard choices America must make if we are to reverse the economic and moral stagnation of the 1980s?

Providing that leadership is not a new mission for the elders in our society. It is a historical role that dates back to early civilizations, when the elders in gerontocratic societies held political and social authority in their societies.[23] That role has been pre-empted over the last 50 years, largely because of our society's orientation toward youth. But that will change. Jones argues that we are seeing the coming "reign of the old" that will bring about "a restoration of the power and the position of the elderly in society"[24] The issue, of course, is what elders will do with that power. Elder leadership has the potential to create a better America if it is used to address the challenges we face, and if elders work with others whose future aging will be affected by what we do or don't do today.

Notes

1. Rauch, J. "Growing old." *National Journal* December 21, 1988, p. 3244.
2. Peterson, P. "The morning after." *The Atlantic Monthly,* October 1987, p. 68.
3. Sowell, T. *Ethnic America.* New York: Basic Books, 1981.
4. Torres-Gil, F. (Ed.). *Hispanics in An Aging Society.* New York: Carnegie Corporation, 1986.
5. Torres-Gil, F. "An examination of factors affecting future cohorts of elderly Hispanics." *The Gerontologist* 26: 140–146.
6. "Many Americans are losing economic ground." *National Journal,* December 10, 1988, p. 3156.
7. Ibid.
8. Rauch, "Growing old."
9. Peterson, "The morning after."
10. U.S. Senate. "Aging America: Trends and Projections: 1987–1988 Edition." Washington, D.C.: U.S. Department of Health and Human Services, 1988.
11. Ibid.
12. Torres-Gil, F. "Interest group politics: Empowerment of the ancianos." In S. Applewhite (Ed.) *Hispanic Elderly in Transition.* Westport Conn.: Greenwood Press, 1988, pp. 75–94.
13. "Nation's elderly are mobilized for the election year." *The Philadelphia Inquirer,* 1988.
14. Kosterlitz, J. "Young vs. old." *National Journal,* December 12, 1988, p. 3160.
15. Chakravarty, S. and K. Weisman. "Consuming our children?" *Forbes,* November 14, 1988, pp. 222–232.

16. Kotkin, J. and Y. Kishimoto. *The Third Century: America's Resurgence in the Asian Era*. New York: Crown Publishers, 1988.

17. Chakravarty and Weisman, "Consuming our children."

18. Cole, T. "The specter of old age: History, politics and culture in an aging America." *Tikkun* 3, 5 (Sept./Oct. 1988): 93–95.

19. Ibid., p. 94.

20. Peterson, "The morning after."

21. Ibid., p. 68.

22. Ibid., p. 69.

23. Jones, L. *Great Expectations: America and the Baby Boom Generation*. New York: Coward, McCann and Geoghegan, 1980.

24. Ibid., p. 325.

CHAPTER SEVEN

Conclusion: Directions for Responsiveness

SCOTT A. BASS, ELIZABETH ANN KUTZA,
AND FERNANDO M. TORRES-GIL

What we have argued in this book is that the greatest change that will occur in the older population in the 1990s and beyond does not involve its size, but its composition. The population will become increasingly diverse. The 69 million elderly who will be alive in the middle of the next century will be more broadly representative in terms of race, socioeconomic status, political beliefs, religious orientation, and health status than ever before.

But we have yet to recognize this new reality or to think about its implications for programs and policies. To date, the aging of our society has been reacted to rather than planned for. As Robert Binstock notes in Chapter 3, undergirding much of public opinion about and public policy toward aging has been an implicit assumption that older persons are relatively homogeneous. Recently, this assumption has led to the pitting of a homogeneous group called "the old" against another group called "the young." Such a view will cause divisiveness, and will, we believe, leave us totally dysfunctional as the older population becomes larger and more diverse.

In the introduction to this book, we observed that the realization that older people are not alike only recently has begun to permeate the public and political consciousnesses. This, we feel, is an important first step. Perhaps it can lead to a renewed acknowledgment of the contributions older persons can make to the larger society. When older persons represent only 10 percent of the population and are seen as all alike, that is, all dependent, there is a tendency to treat them as a special case, a group apart. But when they constitute a quarter of the population, as they are expected to in the next century, their heterogeneity should become obvious and the richness of their experiences perhaps once again may be viewed as a resource for us all.

The next White House Conference on Aging provides a unique opportunity to reflect on the meaning of this diversity and on the challenges and opportunities that it presents. The chapters in this book have examined the impact a diverse older population will have on our political and economic life, and on our service and voluntary sectors. They are meant to provoke discussion and to direct thinking as to how we can successfully respond to such diversity.

Our hope in writing this book was to reach an audience of advocates, program planners, direct service workers, and public policymakers, many of whom will participate in the next White House Conference on Aging. Some will contribute at state or local planning forums; others will journey to Washington, D.C., when the conference officially convenes. We expect that this conference, like its predecessors, will be organized around programmatic areas of service, that is, health, long-term care, and retirement income. But in this book, we have deliberately avoided using such organizing principles and have chosen instead to focus on a theme that over-reaches each of these substantive issues—diversity.

The next White House Conference on Aging must be about change and rightfully should examine diversity. It should grapple with the larger societal constraints that may inhibit appropriate responses to an increasingly diverse older population. And, it should begin to take a "life-course perspective" on how best to ensure that all older persons in the next century will live out long and full natural lives.

A diverse older population will need many things from and will be able to contribute many things to our future society. But to be responsive to these challenges and opportunities, our society and its institutions will have to become knowledgeable, remain flexible, exercise creativity, and be prepared to make some hard choices. It is with this outlook that we identify some residual myths that will have to be dispelled in order for us to successfully plan for the next generation of elders.

Myth 1: Older people share common needs by virtue of their age.

The first step in planning for a future cohort of diverse older persons is an awareness of their diversity. Service professionals, policymakers, and the public need to recognize that "the old" are not a homogeneous group. Older persons are both healthy and ill, or frail. They can no better be characterized as affluent than they can be characterized as poor. They are neither single-mindedly self-interested, nor do they always share the same interests. How we get this message out is of primary importance.

The demographic data reported by Cynthia Taeuber in Chapter 1 is rich in detail. She argues persuasively that the complexities of the elderly's social and economic diversity cannot be understood from sweeping generalizations. And the differences among the subgroups have implications for public policy. Taeuber, like several other authors in this volume, argues for a life-course perspective as we plan for the next generation of seniors, a perspective that recognizes that we age as we have lived. The opportunities and benefits received throughout life determine in large part the circumstances experienced in old age. A changing American profile that includes more minorities, more working women, and more persons who have a history in service occupations will carry with it certain implications for the older population of the next century.

But we cannot begin to think about those implications without knowing the facts. What we need is a mechanism through which the data presented here can be widely disseminated. Both the public and the private sectors can play a part. Groups like the American Association of Retired Persons (AARP) can package these data in such a way that they will be easily understood and widely referenced. The Select Committee on Aging in the House and the Special Committee on Aging in the Senate can be encouraged to develop staff papers for its members to alert them to the heterogeneous nature of the older population. And the Administration on Aging could require that state and area aging plans give greater evidence of a recognition of this diversity. In combination, these mechanisms could sensitize and educate the public, program planners, and policymakers to this new reality among the older population—its diversity.

Information is powerful. It forms the basis on which public opinion is formed and social action taken. Thus, getting out accurate information about the sociodemographic status of older persons is an important first step to successful future planning.

Myth 2: Thanks to the government, all older persons are economically secure in retirement, and the next generation will be even better off than the current one.

It is certainly true that the economic status of older persons is greatly influenced by government provisions for retirement. Social Security benefits are the single largest source of money income for the retiree. As Taeuber notes, since the 1960s, there has been a marked increase in reliance on Social Security. And as benefit levels have outpaced both inflation levels and real wages, these benefits have allowed the economic well-being of older persons to improve.

On the other hand, there has been a decline in the importance of earnings in retirement, even though earnings make a great difference in the economic position of an older person. Thus, rather than predicting an unbroken upward climb in the income position of older persons, some analysts believe that the baby-boom retirees will be less well off than today's retirees. Taeuber reports that personal savings and retirement benefits may be reduced in the future and it is likely that more of the burden for economic security will fall on the individual. Yet many individuals may be unable to carry this burden.

Although the 1980s have given us the longest period of steady economic growth that we have witnessed in several decades, Harry Moody reminds us in Chapter 5 that this should not blind us to several major problems, problems that do not bode well for a prosperous future. His list includes the accumulating federal deficit, our country's adverse trade deficits, and the widening inequality that has occurred in the personal income of individuals. Since 1969, in fact, family household incomes have become more unequal. This phenomenon occurred slowly from 1969 to 1978, accelerated from 1978 to 1982, and has since stabilized.

Since income in retirement is so closely connected to work history, our changing economy may not benefit future seniors. Tomorrow's labor market is likely to have fewer blue-collar workers but greater numbers of pink- (service) and white-collar workers. Advances in transportation and communication have made the world a single marketplace. As a result, labor-intensive activities are likely to be relocated to low-wage Third World countries. Automation will further contract the number of jobs in the production sector while the spreading use of computers may supplant both high- and low-skill white-collar workers. These shifts will affect women and minorities most directly since these groups usually have less education, fewer opportunities for job experience, and are concentrated in relatively low-paying occupations.

The diversity of the older population in the future can counterbalance this troubling scenario, however, if we can see in that diversity what a productive resource an older population can be. Moody believes that such a view will provide a better "fit" in the future.

A sizable number of economists agree with Moody's position and have begun to suggest that it is no longer in the country's economic best interests to encourage the elderly to withdraw from the marketplace. We may need to re-examine the current disincentives to work built into the Social Security program (for example, the earnings limitation on benefits) as well as the provisions in the program that provide an incentive to retire (for example, early retirement benefits). Keeping older persons who can work in the economy will contribute to overall economic growth and at the same time increase tax revenues. (Of course, we must be careful to develop new policies that recognize that not all older persons will be able to remain in the work force. New initiatives must account for this aspect of diversity.)

Another way in which older persons can remain productive is through a National Senior Service Corps, where in return for part-time work, they can receive a stipend. And older persons could use their skills in the market sector of their choice, thus allowing society to utilize the reservoir of their experience for the social good.

Finally, we need to provide training for those who want to continue to work but who may have had limited job experience in their younger years. The older workers' programs sponsored by Private Industry Councils provide us with a model. A requirement of this program, which offers training, placement, and wage subsidy, is that the employer demonstrates a willingness to provide on-the-job training for the upgrading of job skills. A recent solicitation for applicants to this program in Oregon was overwhelmed with responses. The desire and need among the elderly for such opportunities is clearly there.

Through them we can dispel the myth that expects the economic status of the elderly to continue to rise. Future circumstances may not produce such an optimistic scenario unless we actively develop programs that will re-engage older persons as productive contributors to the economy and to their own economic futures.

Myth 3: Intergenerational equity issues will continue to provoke conflict between the aged and the young.

It is time to reframe our conventional aging policy debate with its emphasis on redistribution. So argues Moody in Chapter 5. He calls attention to the set of assumptions that underlie most current discussions of aging policy, assumptions that he says can be summed up in a single phrase: the elderly are a needy population. Once granted that assumption, what follows is a decision as to which other group in society will pay for the benefits that this needy group will claim. It is now presumed that the young will have to bear this burden, to their future disadvantage. Another part of these assumptions is that there is a fixed pie from which such redistribution must occur.

We would like to argue that this set of assumptions bears re-examination. First, if in the next century, American society develops programs that will encourage the continued productive contribution of its elderly members, then the resource pie will not remain fixed. Older producers can help enlarge the pie and create new resources. This shift in thinking, as Moody describes it, begins to move us away from seeing older people exclusively as a needy population or as a "burden" to society; instead we see older persons as a resource in an *interdependent* society.

This theme of intergenerational "interdependence" is reinforced by Fernando Torres-Gil and Mimi Kmet in Chapter 6. They propose that older persons themselves are best positioned to provide a new kind of political leadership in the next century. This leadership will not be directed at promoting their own short-term self-interest (more government benefits), but at promoting policies that will serve the interests of future generations of elderly who are now young. As these authors eloquently state, "Who better to lobby and fight for increased funding for education and health care, and for increased revenues to reduce the federal deficit, which, if left unattended, will be the fiscal legacy for their children and grandchildren? Who better than the influential aging organizations to develop alliances with groups representing minorities and children to fight for prenatal programs and day care for single mothers?" Providing this leadership will reposition older persons in the role of elder statesmen and stateswomen, encouraging, through the strength of their wisdom and moral authority, the development of policies that will serve future generations. It is this vision that will set aside future intergenerational conflict, and it is this vision that we should work toward.

Myth 4: Services for older persons should be national in administration and standardized in their operation across the country.

Since the New Deal, it has been a cherished belief among political liberals that public benefits to individuals should be provided through national programs with standardized program operations. Yet acceptance of the notion of heterogeneity of circumstances and need may argue for just the opposite—more creative, locally controlled programs.

The need for service programs that are responsive to a wide range of diverse needs brings us once again into an old debate, specifically, the debate as to which level of government should be responsible for social programs. Our constitutional protection of states' rights leads Elizabeth Kutza in Chapter 4 to believe that totally nationalizing our social programs is not to be expected. For both fiscal and constitutional reasons, she argues that there is likely to remain a sharing of program responsibility. Of course, it is clear that the federal government has the greater flexibility and capacity to raise revenues, and that leaving all social program responsibility to lower levels of government has and will lead to troubling interstate disparities.

But recently, instead of discussing how responsibility for programs should be shared among all levels of government, there has been an abdication of responsibility at all levels. Federal, state, and local governmental officials alike have been cutting back on their offer of many services, and have been reluctant to raise new revenues to support a growing demand. New taxes are unpopular, yet citizens in our modern society face many needs that can only be provided under public auspices. Therefore, as we face new demands from an increasingly diverse older population, we must re-engage in the time-worn debate concerning *which* level of government should bear *which* burdens for *which* social programs.

For some, the tendency will be to say that the federal government should take over major responsibility in all areas. Yet this singular alternative has some peculiar problems when we are facing a population with diverse needs. For example, a common, yet unfortunate companion to federal funding is often a rigid and inflexible set of administrative rules. Kutza uses a vignette to illustrate this point. In most federal programs that fund homemaker/home health aide care, such care can be delivered only through a formal agency. Payment cannot be made to available neighbors or family members. Yet a rural area may have no such formal agencies. These general rules are clearly unresponsive to local circumstances. Many states have recognized this and, through their own supplemental funding, allow for client-employed helpers to be paid with public funds. One question that needs answering, then, is how we can ensure that large national or state programs remain flexible enough to allow for local administrative discretion.

Yet the words "administrative discretion" raise considerable concern among social welfare professionals. American social welfare history, in fact, is a history of efforts to *limit* discretion of program operations. As Kutza notes, too many abuses of individual civil rights have accompanied such discretion. But perhaps the time has come to reassess this issue so we can develop diverse service responses to diverse service needs.

Sanford Kravitz, Martha Pelaez, and Max Rothman note in Chapter 2 that the growing racial and multicultural configuration of the elderly population raises further questions about the service sectors' capacity to respond. How can services be developed that are culturally sensitive? We need to guard against older persons refusing to participate in programs that they need because of the existence of linguistic or cultural barriers.

Diversity also may require us to become more creative about the targeting of social programs. In Chapter 3, Binstock raises the issue of targeting and argues that there is nothing technically difficult about it. Rather, the matter is whether programs that are targeted can enjoy any political support. He is skeptical about aged-based mass membership organizations becoming partners in re-examination of the targeting issue, but he believes that they should. In contrast, Moody calls for a reframing of the issue of allocating benefits and eschews engaging in the targeting debate. But the targeting issue is likely to become increasingly important as the aged population becomes more diverse.

Dispelling these four myths will not be easy. But the opportunity to do so is presented to us by the next White House Conference on Aging. This most important national forum can be a vehicle through which the theme of diversity is introduced into the public consciousness, and in which new programs can be developed that respond to this diversity. We firmly believe that diversity in aging is *the* issue of the 1990s and beyond.

During the next several decades, we envision the growth of an aging society whose diversity presents both opportunities and challenges. There will be an excitement accompanying the aging process, as individuals see old age not as inevitable decline, but merely as another life stage with opportunities for growth, learning, and community participation.

But as it may liberate, diversity also complicates. It calls upon society to exhibit a greater sensitivity and responsiveness to the needs of older individuals who vary widely in all dimensions—gender, age, income, health, and education. It requires flexibility on the part of our social institutions, a flexibility often incompatible with organizations and their rules. And it requires a political willingness to look beyond the least common denominator of political demands toward policies that can benefit individuals in these varying circumstances.

Our hope in writing this book is that we will begin to reflect on this diversity in our aging society and formulate a compassionate and constructive response for the 1990s and beyond.

Index